The
MEDITATION
Yearbook

52 MEDITATIONS
FOR A YEAR OF MINDFULNESS,
CONNECTION & INNER PEACE

JOEY HULIN

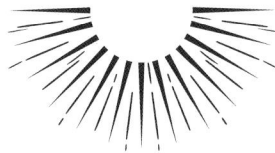

DAVID & CHARLES
—PUBLISHING—

www.davidandcharles.com

CONTENTS

The
MEDITATION
Yearbook

INTRODUCTION

Meditation is a practice where science and mysticism meet. It has deep roots in history, spirituality, religion and culture, and it's rich in philosophy, ritual and tradition. It is also a practice deeply valued by modern science, with a growing body of peer-reviewed research proving the incredible benefits meditation has on all aspects of mental health and wellbeing.

In essence, meditation is a way of getting to know yourself more intimately, even through the simplest of practices. It is in stillness, quietly sitting with ourselves without distraction, that we get to know our inner world of thoughts, feelings and emotions. Through mindfulness and physical awareness, we are able to understand the language of the body and harmonise communication between mind, body and spirit. Through movement meditations and sound practices, we are able to enter trance-like states, transcending the mind and reaching deeper states of consciousness. As a meditation practice deepens, we become familiar with our spiritual essence. We might feel a deeper sense of connection with nature, energy and forces much bigger than ourselves. Through regular meditation practice, we become more of who we truly are.

There is no one way to practise meditation and no practice that is superior to another. Each brings with them unique traits, benefits, instructions and a set of possibilities. You can see this book as a box of chocolates, offering a taste of a number of meditation approaches. Some you'll enjoy more than others. Some you'll find helpful today, but by next year may be another will be more useful. Meditation always meets us where we are.

There are 52 meditations within this yearbook, one for every week of the year, separated into six different categories: spiritual connection, nature connection, mind-body-spirit, movement, true self and mindful living. Within each meditation, you'll find an introduction that outlines the history, the benefits and the intention of the practice. You will then find a 'how to', offering simple guidance to allow you to practise at home. Finally, there is a personal reflection from me, offering you an honest, raw and candid insight into my own experience of each meditation or my thoughts and reflections on the theme around it.

How to use this book

You can work through this book in several ways. You might choose to systematically move through the book, reading and practising one meditation over the course of each week, for the duration of the year. You might choose to read through all the meditations in this book in one go, gobbling up the guidance, and from there deciding which meditation you would like to try first. You may wish to glance through the meditation titles and select a meditation that best suits your needs right now. Or you may choose to use it as a divination process, opening a page at random and letting the book decide what you need. Either way, let this journey be about playful curiosity and exploration. See each meditation as a path back home to yourself and your true nature, and be kind to yourself as you go.

AWAKEN

Spiritual Connection Meditations

Spiritual meditations help you make sense of life and help you understand your place in the world, bringing with them a swelling feeling of comforting relief.

The Meditations

Are you ready to dive deep and explore the wild and mystical realm of spiritual meditation? In this chapter, you will begin a transcendent journey, exploring otherworldly realms and your subconscious mind. You will train your focus, befriend the present moment, meet spirit guides, remember your true nature and recall lost wisdom, all to help awaken you to a divine energy that is always available to you, and is found within.

There is a growing number of people who identify as 'spiritual but not religious', perhaps you are one of them? Exploring and practising spiritual meditations such as Zen, Kundalini, Celtic and Shamanic practices doesn't require you to believe a certain way or pledge allegiance to a particular doctrine or religion. Giving yourself the freedom to explore various spiritual approaches, philosophies and practices, allows you to take what resonates and leave what doesn't. You may stumble across something that speaks to you on a profoundly deep level and decide to explore that particular path in greater depth. Spiritual meditations help you make sense of life and understand your place in the world, bringing with them a swelling feeling of comforting relief. Remembering that no one approach or practice is more effective, better or evolved than another is particularly important when exploring spirituality. Ultimately, all paths lead to the same destination.

Defining 'spiritual' can be a tricky task. It can be a loaded or intimidating term for some or it might be associated with one particular organised religion for others. We tend to believe our own definition, and that's the way it should be. But for our exploration here, however, let's see if we can approach these meditations with a beginner's mind, using the following definition to steer us.

Let's assume that spirituality is a visceral belief that this human experience is more than just mind and matter, and that we are a part of, and influenced by, something unseen that is much greater than ourselves. Spiritual meditations help us connect with an energy, life force or spirit that resides within all things, leading to a feeling of awakening. For some, awakening is the process of ascending upwards, through higher levels of consciousness towards liberation and freedom from suffering. Other approaches explain it as rooting down, descending into and integrating the imaginal and the subconscious mind. Science might suggest that it all has to do with accessing brain wave states.

Explore, play, try things on for size. Choose what feels right, clean and soothing, leave what feels confusing or jarring. Trust yourself and choose a path or a practice that helps you to *be love*.

SHAMANIC MEDITATION
Journey Within

The cross-cultural roots of Shamanism are so rich, it could be said they penetrate the whole globe: from Inuit tribes to Indonesia, from the Amazon to Australia, South America to Africa and ancient Britain to Siberia. Evidence of shamanic practices appears in all ancient cultures[1], predating any organised religion. Although it is a lost way of life in many modern cultures, for many native cultures around the world, it is still an established cultural practice today.

Shamanism is a way of life, one that deeply honours the interconnection of us humans with nature, the mysteries of the spirit world and the power of the subconscious mind. Community-based rituals, rites of passage and ceremonies are vitally important in shamanism, while most shamanic philosophies and practices point towards self-healing. Sometimes referred to as a medicine woman or medicine man, a Shaman is a healer or guide who acts as a bridge or mediator between the spirit world (or the unconscious mind) and the physical world (the conscious mind).

Journeying is a shamanic meditation practice that engages the active imagination of the subconscious mind and the spiritual realm. A shamanic journey is a trance-like meditative state that often involves working with spirit guides, ancestors or nature, allowing you to go on an internal journey to return to wholeness, and to access your own inner wisdom. Although some shamanic cultures use psychedelic plant medicines in ceremonies to induce altered states, it is not always the case. Altered states of consciousness and trance-like states are often brought about by drumming, music, chanting or dancing.

Benefits: *Promotes emotional healing; processes experiences; shifts creative, emotional and physical blocks; clears stagnant energy; connects you with spirit guides*

Key features: *Working with the subconscious mind, allowing you to daydream, receive visions or meet spirit guides*

Length: *20 minutes to 1 hour*

Frequency: *Weekly/monthly*

Tools: *Smudging sage or other native herbs, a drum or drumming music, blanket and a timer*

Best practised: *With a guide (Shaman) to lead the journey in ceremony, but it can also be a self-led practise experienced at home*

It is in the meditative state when the mind becomes more creative and what is stored in the subconscious mind becomes more accessible. There is nothing you need to do to 'journey' but simply trust, let go and surrender into the lucid dream of the subconscious mind. Let images, visualisations and memories come and go without effort to control, reject or analyse them. Hand over control of the mind's grip and trust the stirrings of the subconscious mind, allowing your own inner wisdom to guide you. This grants permission for the magical realm of the subconscious to process emotions, experiences and memories. You might emerge feeling realigned, cleansed and whole.

How to practise this meditation at home

Prepare: This is an important element of shamanic practices. Ensure you are in a safe and comfortable spot for your meditative journey. You might like to cleanse your space by smudging with sage or other native herbs. Dim the lights and cover yourself with a blanket. Set a timer. Lie back and let go.

Step one: Choose an intention for the direction of travel for your journey. Invite the subconscious mind (or Spirit) to guide you to meet a spirit guide, spirit animal or an ancestor, for example. But remain open to wherever the visions take you.

Step two: Take a few moments to focus on your breath, become present, anchored fully into the reality of the present moment before you begin. Look around the space you are in and feel the rhythmic beat of your own heart. Consciously connect to the life force of nature and of you. Send gratitude to your spirit guides, ancestors and nature for supporting you. Bring your intention back to mind.

Step three: Press play on the drumming music, or begin slowly drumming yourself, gently building up, allowing the rhythm to move itself. Close your eyes and rest back into your meditation. Relax the body and allow the rhythm of the drum to guide you. Drift and dream.

Close: When the timer sounds, or when it feels right to end your meditation, re-engage with the sensations within and around the physical body. Feel your body, mind, heart and spirit become more present in the physical reality. Stop playing the recording or gently draw your drumming to a close. Feel present in the physical surroundings but keep your eyes closed and sit in silence for a few moments. Allow an integration of all that unfolded consciously and subconsciously during your meditation. Take a big energising breath in and open your eyes.

Reflection

I remember reading a chapter in a brilliant book called *The Lotus and the Lily*, many years ago, in which author Janet Connor invites readers to 'be your own Shaman'. I remember the invitation not landing quite right with me at the time. What even is a Shaman? Aren't they chosen or special? How could I possibly be my own? A few years later the penny dropped. I understood what she meant, and it is the very same sentiment any authentic Shaman will teach too: the real power and magic is the healer within, not the guide or the tool. It is the body, mind and spirit's natural ability to return to a state of wholeness, given the right conditions. The role of a Shaman is to act as a guide, a mediator between worlds, and to hold space for the self-healer within to activate. It is their role to remind us of this, to open up a channel back home to ourselves and to remember the truth of our inherent wholeness. This power doesn't lie in another's authority because you are the potential, you are the life force, you are Spirit. Therefore, through the use of daily rituals, intentions, meditation and conscious choices, in your own simple, daily life, you can be your own Shaman.

CELTIC MEDITATION
Make Life Sacred

The Celts sought out the sacred in just about all aspects of their daily lives. They engaged in dance, seasonal living and seasonal celebrations, honouring sacred sites, attuned to nature and honoured deities, gods and goddesses to deepen their connection to life. They experienced the divine through nature and saw life itself as a cause for celebration. Living in harmony with the seasons allowed them to connect on a deeper level to the spirit that resided in all things, including themselves. They believed in mother god, alchemy, magic and natural healing. They worshipped the earth, the sun, the moon and the stars, alongside some deities, gods and goddesses who they believed ruled the skies and seasons. The Celts believed in the importance of harmony and balance between masculine and feminine energies too, and held space for both men and women in roles of community and spiritual leadership.

The Celts had a prayer for nearly all aspects of daily life, such as collecting kindling, planting, harvesting, eating and fire-lighting. There is a beautiful Celtic ritual called the breastplate prayer, which is the practice of dressing yourself in grace, through prayer, as well as with clothes in the morning[2].

Meditation was used to honour the physical realm, to deepen their understanding of the needs of the physical world and connect to the sacredness of it. This planet is magnificent, after all. But isn't this an interesting contrast to most other spiritual practices, where meditation is used to connect with the spiritual world, not the physical one?

Benefits: *Helps with grounding and to experience clarity; promotes present-moment awareness; evokes gratitude and appreciation; celebrates simple things*

Key features: *Connecting with nature and celebrating seasons with ritual and ceremony*

Length: *Moment by moment/any*

Frequency: *Daily*

Tools: *Offerings*

Best practised: *Out in nature or at a sacred site*

Meditation was a way to set up for magic, to cast spells and to pray. They also used the shamanistic meditation technique of journeying to connect more deeply to the spirit world. A Celtic meditation is a living, breathing meditation that is woven throughout the mundane, daily happenings of life – a conscious choice to worship.

To make life sacred, say a prayer for everything, whisper thank you to Mother Earth for the glass of water you drink, the food you eat, the shelter you live underneath, and the family you share yourself and your life with. Be present to the seasons as they change and life itself becomes a meditation.

How to practise this meditation at home

Prepare: If it's possible, try this Celtic-inspired meditation at a Celtic sacred site. If not, then at an old tree, or simply get out in nature in your garden or your nearest beach, park or forest. Take with you an offering as a physical manifestation of gratitude and respect. This might be perishable food items, it might be flowers, or it could be a poem or letter of thanks.

Step one: Settle down to a seated position, directly on the earth and place your offering next to you. Close your eyes and consciously connect with the energy of the place. Remember the ancient lineage of people, animals, plants, elements and spirits who have passed through that very site.

Step two: Feel down into the earth and remember the web of roots and life connecting beneath, and give thanks for the earth that sustains and nourishes life. If you are at a human-made sacred site, honour the intentional placing of the sacred site, aligning with the stars above and connecting to the earth below. If at a natural site, honour the will and persistence of nature to adapt, live seasonally and thrive. Connect with the pulse of life force moving through all living things and the poetry of it.

Close: Become present to the same life force moving through you and give thanks for it. When you are ready, slowly open your eyes and take your time to become aware of your surroundings, anchoring yourself back into the present moment.

Reflection

I was born and raised in the British Isles where, all my life, I've experienced a thirst, a longing, for a greater sense of connection to the ancient native cultures of this land. I live in west Cornwall where the remains of stone circles, quoits and many other mystical structures, wells and mounds still stand, often hidden down bramble-lined tracks. History tells us the Romans gave up their effort to conquer the far southwest of England because of its remoteness. Instead, they simply staked a claim over the land.

This disinterest in the west has allowed glimpses of our Celtic culture to remain, weathered, yet rooted in the earth. I had a profound moment one day when I was on my knees seeking guidance. So often we look up to the skies – out there – and ask 'Please, something/someone, help me'. Instead, I felt a call to draw my prayer down to the earth, to pray to mother god. The energy of my whole body shifted as I asked Mother Nature for guidance; suddenly I didn't feel alone. My body and my heart became more present. I drew my prayer in closer and I asked the universe within for guidance. Suddenly praying felt right. The visceral shift that occurred felt ancient, unearthing glimpses of the weathered remains of my own knowing rooted within.

VIPASSANA MEDITATION
Gain Clarity

Vipassana meditation, sometimes referred to as 'insight meditation', is one of India's oldest formal meditation techniques. It translates as 'to see things clearly' or 'to see things as they really are'. It is a foundational form of mindfulness. The Buddha, Siddhartha Gautama, achieved enlightenment through the practice of Vipassana. As the story goes, he spent many years practising various forms of meditation, he studied books, kissed the feet of gurus, he tried and tested all spiritual practices available to him in search of relief and enlightenment. Some provided momentary relief, but before too long a lingering sense of suffering and seeking would return. One day, weary from his spiritual quest, he surrendered. He sat down under a fig tree, later referred to as a bodhi tree, and for 49 days he meditated, abstaining from movement or food – 49 days of silence, stillness, abstinence. When he emerged, he experienced a permanent state of inner liberation and freedom from suffering. He arrived at an ultimate truth about life, and Self, that freedom and liberation aren't found in a practice or a guru, but instead, it is found within. He had become enlightened.

A Vipassana meditation practice involves silence, structure, abstinence and the cultivation of non-judgement through self-observation. It is often taught in a retreat setting for, most commonly, ten days. During this ten-day retreat, you abstain from speaking, reading, writing, entertainment of any kind, technology, eye contact or physical contact. Instead, practitioners spend most of the day in silent meditation. Retreats can last months or even years. Some Buddhist monks commit to a lifetime of this practice. The essence of this – silence, seated, expanded awareness – forms the foundation of an at-home Vipassana practice.

Benefits: *Offers psychological clarity and focus; helps with present-moment awareness; develops self-discipline; helps find inner peace*

Key features: *Using masculine energy to expand awareness and observe thoughts and feelings*

Length: *Build up from 5 minutes to, ideally, 40 minutes*

Frequency: *Daily*

Tools: *A cushion, a blanket or shawl for your shoulders and a timer*

Best practised: *On a ten-day silent retreat*

A growing amount of research shows that the long term effects of a regular practice of Vipassana meditation increases feelings of general wellbeing and compassion, decreases emotional reactivity and suggests changes in self-experience of life itself[3]. This change in self-experience of life is key to a Vipassana practice. The ability to sit with ourselves, to notice what is there and to transcend it, helps us to realise we are not our thoughts, feelings, emotions or even behaviours but the one who observes them. This ability to see clearly helps us make informed choices and rewire negative habits, lifestyle choices and thought patterns. Whether it leads to enlightenment or not, you'll have to put your bottom on a cushion to find out.

How to practise this meditation at home

Prepare: Ensure you have a decent length of time to practise, ideally 40 minutes. Place a cushion on the floor and sit in a crossed-legged position. Cover your shoulder with a blanket. Set a timer for 40 minutes and shut your eyes.

Step one: Notice the content of your mind. What thoughts and distractions are present for you? See if you can notice this content as the curious, loving observer of your thoughts, creating some space between you and them.

Step two: Start to move your awareness, like a body scan, from the top of your head to your toes, working a different way around your body each time you scan. Notice the sensations in each part of the body objectively. Notice what is there rather than trying to change anything. Sitting for a long period of time will undoubtedly cause the body to speak to you in various ways. This, according to the practice, is part of what is meant to be transcended. But go carefully, making sure not to hurt yourself.

Close: When the timer sounds, take a deep breath and bring your awareness back to your body once more. Allow any physical or mental frustrations to ease away. Evoke feelings of kindness and compassion to all beings before opening your eyes.

Reflection

Seven days into a ten-day Vipassana retreat, lower back aching, body stiff from the lack of movement, I experienced a surge of energy that seemed to surface from the depths of me. Sitting in silence with myself for seven days hadn't been the challenge I was hoping for. I was hoping to explore the murky depth of my subconscious and to face my shadow. Instead, this whoosh of energy was a surge of suppressed joy. A bubbling of creativity, excitement and a willingness to live, love and enjoy life wanted to burst through. It took all my might to not stand up and wail a song, strip my clothes off and run naked through the fields! I was alive and this surge of feminine energy felt naughty, almost fairy-like, and wanted to be expressed. The masculine energy that held the retreat together – structure, routine, discipline, order, cleanliness, silence, rules – revealed to me the suppressed wild feminine energy that was longing to be expressed. To move, flow, be messy, dance, sing, laugh, look others in the eyes, hug them, listen to them. Something about the extended silence made me glimpse the truth of who I really am and the gift that this life is to be lived.

ZEN MEDITATION
Find Focus

Zen, also known as Zazen, meditation is a goalless meditation practice from the Zen Buddhist tradition. With some meditation approaches, you set an intention before entering into the practice, perhaps to reduce stress, meet a spirit guide or deepen a spiritual connection. A Zen meditation requires the opposite – to arrive empty of expectations and to just simply sit. The multitude of benefits a practitioner might experience are merely a result of, not a reason for, meditation. In our goal-oriented modern world, this concept of simply being can feel, well, uncomfortable! How do you empty yourself out? How do you rid yourself of preconceptions and demands? How do you stop that busy old mind of yours from thinking, thinking, thinking? A Zen monk's answer would be – with Zen meditation.

Zen meditation is an offshoot of Buddhism and is often interchangeably understood alongside Vipassana and mindfulness. It could be argued that all are, in some ways, different sides to the same coin. Buddhist meditations, including Zen, are concerned with present-moment awareness, becoming the observer of the mind and cultivating non-judgement and compassion. Zen philosophy has a vivid analogy to bring this to life with the metaphor of the 'monkey mind', where thoughts are seen as wild monkeys causing havoc, swinging around in the mind with a lot of commotion and noise. The purpose of Zen meditation is to befriend and tame the monkeys of the mind (thoughts and distractions), not to punish or fight against them – that only contributes to the chaos. It is through the practice of Zen meditation that we create a safe space within ourselves to sit and observe the 'monkey mind', without judgement. In doing so, calmness and order naturally arise.

Benefits: *Helps focus and train attention; develops self-discipline; quiets racing thoughts; provides an antidote to screen time; raises energy levels*

Key features: *Using structured, masculine energy to expand awareness and observe thoughts and feelings, and to observe the breath*

Length: *5 to 10 minutes*

Frequency: *Daily, first thing in the morning*

Tools: *A cushion, a meditation chime and a timer*

Best practised: *Facing a wall!*

Research has found that Zen meditation activates a part of the brain called the default mode network in the brains of regular Zen meditators[4]. This part of the brain is responsible for focus, attention and concentration, and stops the mind from becoming overwhelmed or overstimulated. So we have yet another example of science catching up with what ancient teachings already knew.

How to practise this meditation at home

There are very clear instructions on how to set yourself up for a Zen meditation, including a way to sit, rest your hands and enter into meditation. Follow the steps below to try it for yourself at home.

Prepare: Set a timer for 10 or 15 minutes, preferably in the morning, to practise. Sit in an upright, crossed-legged position on the floor on a cushion (or sit upright on a chair if sitting on the floor is not possible for you).

Step one: Ensure your spine is upright, straight and tall. The reason you are required to be upright and seated, rather than lying down, is to not relax too much, to remain conscious and alert throughout your meditation. There is a Zen saying that explains by sitting in this way, you are 'a tiger ready to pounce, not a sleeping pig'. With a straight spine, tuck your chin in slightly to extend the back of the neck, creating a straight line from the tailbone up to the crown of the head. Soften your shoulders and belly.

Step two: Place your right palm facing up in your lap, then place the left palm, also facing up, into the palm of the right hand, and allow the thumbs to slightly touch. This mudra, or hand position, is said to allow the flow of energy to move freely around the body.

Step three: Keep your eyes slightly open, just a fraction. Let your gaze be soft and lowered, not focusing on anything in particular.

Step four: Breathe easily, through the nose, without control. Allow your awareness to rest on your breath, using it as an anchor of focus for the duration of your meditation. If your mind wanders, simply return to your breath. This cycle of losing focus and then returning is the essence of this meditation.

Close: Take a long, deep breath and open your eyes.

Reflection

My alarm sounds at 5.30am. I rub the sleep from my eyes and roll out of bed straight onto a meditation cushion that I had dutifully laid out ready the night before. I light a candle (which is not traditionally part of a Zen routine but something that helps me anchor into meditation). I set a timer on my phone for 10 minutes, take a deep breath and lower my gaze. Being too entangled with our thoughts can be the root cause of anxiety and depression. Both, as most of us know, have a physiological effect on our body, and our general sense of wellbeing. Through Zen meditation we are able to figuratively sit back into the seat of awareness and observe our thoughts, to untangle ourselves from them to realise we are not them. With practice, the self-observation, non-judgement, non-attachment and compassion that is experienced while seated on a meditation cushion, can be embodied and lived out in everyday life through a mindfulness practice. The timer sings, to signal the end of my meditation and the start of my day. A simple, understated practice that has become my anchor to presence, able then to notice all the magic the universe lays out for me each day.

MANTRA MEDITATION
Experience Bliss

There is something undeniably hypnotic about mantras. Whether they are listened to or recited, either silently in your mind or chanted out loud, the melodic repetition of a word or phrase somehow seems to naturally soothe busy minds, evoke powerful emotions and induce feelings of calm and bliss.

The word mantra translates from Sanskrit as 'mind tool' – *mans* meaning mind and *tra* meaning tool. In English, it is referred to as a chant. Mantra meditation can be traced back thousands of years to the Vedic period in India, some 1000 years BC. Mantras were used as a meditative tool for connecting with divine energy, leading to transcendence. Since then, chanting has been a spiritual practice present in almost all organised religions. The transcendental sounds of Gregorian chants from the 8th and 9th centuries or the enchanting magic of chanting Tibetan monks are sweet-sounding examples. A growing amount of research is proving that chanting reduces stress, lowers anxiety, improves sleep, and leads to better social cohesion[5]. Through studying the brains of mantra meditators, neurophysiologists have found that meditative chanting activates an area of the brain associated with brain waves that link to deep sleep and amnesia[6]. Even humming is said to have a calming effect on the vagus nerve, the main component of our 'rest and digest' parasympathetic nervous system. Meditative chanting or reciting mantras acts like a vehicle to transport us deeper into meditation and closer to divine energy.

Two mantra meditation approaches popular today are Vedic meditation and Transcendental Meditation (TM). Both require you to attend teacher-led sessions, who assign you a personal mantra. The ancient practice of Vedic meditation requires meditators to practise for a set amount of time every day – 20 minutes in the morning and 20 minutes in the evening. For the

Benefits: *Aids relaxation; helps to transcend thoughts; calms the nervous system; improves sleep; attends to spiritual alignment*

Key features: *Surrendering to monotonous sound to create spiritual connection*

Length: *Any*

Frequency: *Daily*

Tools: *Timer*

Best practised: *In community circles*

duration of your meditation, you recite your assigned mantra either silently in your mind or out loud. Transcendental Meditation was developed much more recently in the late 1950s by Maharishi Mahesh Yogi, and quickly became a popular meditation amongst celebrities. You have to attend training for TM, often with a rather large price tag, in order to learn and be assigned your mantra. The mantras given, often just a sound, are influenced by your age, gender or other determining physical factors. However, the broader landscape of mantra meditation, which is plentiful and rich, doesn't require formal training. It is a simple, easily accessible meditation practice you can do at home.

How to practise this meditation at home

Prepare: Choose a mantra for yourself – a word or phrase that feels the most significant to you at this particular time in your life. You can select something from your native language or you can work with Sanskrit words, which are claimed to hold more vibrational resonance with the universe. You might like to use *'om'* or the Sanskrit word for peace – *'shanti'*. English words that feel powerful to work with include: 'I am loved', 'I am enough', 'I am held', 'I am safe' and 'I am peace'. You might also choose to find a piece of chanting music or a recording of a Sanskrit mantra to listen to for the duration of your meditation. For this meditation, I'll guide you using a Sanskrit phrase, *so-hum*. *So-hum* is a Hindu mantra that translates as 'I am'.

When you are ready to begin your meditation, set a timer for however long you have to practise, ten to fifteen minutes is always good.

Step one: Settle the breath and allow the body to come into stillness. As you inhale, repeat your mantra in your mind and again on the out breath. If you've chosen a mantra with more than one word, use one part of your mantra on the inhale and the rest on the out breathe. For example, breathe in and repeat *'so'* silently in your mind, and as you breath out repeat *'hum'*.

Step two: Perform this monotonous repetition for the duration of the meditation.

Close: When the timer sounds, drop the repetition and allow the mind to relax, noticing the vast expanse of silent space that opens up.

Reflection

One of my first spiritual teachers was an ex-ordained Buddhist monk who had left behind her robes and shaved head for a quiet life in Cornwall with her husband, her hair now flowing. Her teachings felt unique and enticing, they seemed to lift a veil to a view of an endless horizon filled with metaphysical possibilities and wonder, yet rooted in a firm foundation of Buddhist philosophy. She mentored me over several years, giving me permission to dream big, to reach for the stars and to befriend the present moment. She would say, '100 per cent intention, 100 per cent surrender'. Sat in her small back bedroom, turned meditation room, we meditated with the mantra *'so-hum'*. Breathing in the endless possibilities – *'so'*. Breathing out the earthy safety of presence – *'hum'*. The sky felt like it opened up above me. A channel of energy and light poured down, and through me, as my body became the earth. Hypnotised by the repetition – *so-hum, so-hum, so-hum* – I experienced bliss.

DEVOTIONAL MEDITATION
Be Inspired

Devotional meditation involves holding someone or something outside of yourself in your meditation, in order to gain a deeper sense of spiritual connection. Some spiritual seekers might have a devotional practice to certain gurus, goddesses, deities, prophets or saints. Nature herself might be at the centre of devotion.

Devotional practices can be found in spiritual traditions dotted all over the world. Bhakti yoga, otherwise known as devotional yoga, focuses on loving devotion to a personal deity. Pagan devotional practices involve creating altars, bringing the natural world in (for example, the Christmas tree or wreath), or laying offerings out in nature in gratitude. The Balinese have a beautiful devotional practice where, every morning they create trays out of banana leaves in silent meditation, often as a family, and fill them with treats, such as rice, flowers, fruit and incense and leave them out for the gods. Devotional practices are active forms of meditation, acknowledging the divine in someone or something and seeing that as a portal to a deeper sense of spiritual connection.

Generally, meditation could be seen as synonymous with introspection, self-healing, self-regulation and other such personal benefits, a focus which I'd argue is desperately required in our over-stressed, disconnected modern culture. But personal health and wellbeing aren't where the power of meditation ends. Devotional practices such as prayer offer us a practice for holding others in our thoughts and hearts, while reiki is a powerful healing technique where a trained professional enters into a meditative state to become a channel for healing for another person.

Benefits: *Boosts a sense of belonging, purpose and community connection; increases confidence and feelings of support; a feel-good practice*

Key features: *To see potential, love and the divine in someone or something and honour this*

Length: *5 to 10 minutes*

Frequency: *Daily, first thing in the morning*

Tools: *An altar or shrine, a candle and incense*

Best practised: *At a simple altar at home*

Devotional meditation can evoke feelings of gratitude, appreciation, love and respect for something outside of ourselves. It is highly individual and personal, and can be seen as a yummy, feel-good meditation for you to enjoy, and for others to energetically benefit from. A devotional practice isn't about worship. It's not about becoming more like someone else but instead to recognise the light, love, power and divinity in something or someone else, in order to bring you closer to your own divine essence.

How to practise this meditation at home

Prepare: Spend some time in quiet reflection, or journal your thoughts out onto a page, reflecting on what or who helps you feel closer to your own personal sense of spirit or the divine. Is there something or somewhere in nature, or someone who feels like they bring out the light in you? It could be an animal, an ancestor, a place, a friend, a mentor or a child. It's fun to consider who or what, even spending some time reflecting on this can evoke feelings of love and connection.

Step one: Place a photo, image or objects associated with your devotional muse, along with a candle and some incense, in a quiet corner of your home. For nature-based shrines, collect seasonal plants, leaves, berries or herbs, which can be replenished and replaced seasonally. The focal point of pagan meditation practices often involves a shrine or altar. Go to your altar daily to begin your meditation.

Step two: Ritualistically light a candle before your devotional meditation, with the intention of connecting with the place, person or thing you are devoting your practice to. Hold it or them in mind as you light the candle.

Step three: Close your eyes, take a few centring deep breaths and hold the essence of the place, person or thing in your heart for the duration of the meditation. Notice how emotions surface and evolve. Allow whatever wants to surface, to surface.

Close: When you are ready, finish your meditation by opening your eyes and blowing out the candle.

Reflection

If we look closely enough, most people today are living devotionally, centring things on the physical world as something to worship, things that don't give back in a spiritual sense, unable to close the loop. Are people now devoted to their phones, to money, to power, to accumulating material possessions to the detriment of their mental and spiritual health? Can the spirit or the divine be found in those things? They sure feel like blocks to me, things that keep me in a numbed state, boxed in, not good enough, where peace always seems just out of reach. I've played with this practice a lot over the years, devoting my meditation to different things; the children in my life/my dog/the tree I would climb as a child/the ocean/to goddess Diana/to Shakti. In doing so, my heart seems to swell in my chest and I become alert in presence. Through them, I am reminded of my own innocence, power, vulnerability, playfulness and potential. Love becomes a portal to the divine.

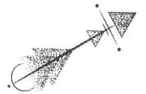

SACRED SCRIPTURES MEDITATION
Uncover Meaning

Words written from a place of truth and feeling hold so much power. This is a phenomenon that has been recognised and understood throughout time. Whether it's the feelings poetry or prose evoke, or the sense of closeness to spirit experienced when reading a religious or spiritual text. Words contain so much more than just letters. They are alive, plump and overflowing with meaning and feeling. There is a wonderful phrase and practice in Latin that describes this phenomenon – *Lectio Divina*, which means 'divine reading'. The practice of *Lectio Divina* teaches that words contain feeling, magic and energy that can reveal deeper truths about ourselves and life. Isn't it interesting how sometimes a word or sentence, hidden in a sea of words, will pop out at you and make you take notice? It is as if the energy of that word or phrase resonates with you on a deeper, subconscious level.

Traced back to the third century, *Lectio Divina* is a Christian monastic practice involving sacred scriptures for meditation, contemplation and communion with God. Words and passages are read as a means of feeling and viscerally understanding the spiritual meaning, rather than cognitively analysing them. It is thought that meaning is hidden within the words, a deep wisdom that might be passed on without intention. When you meditate on words, phrases, passages or readings, their meaning comes to life.

Lectio Divina is commonly taught in four stages: read, meditate, pray and contemplate. I see this process almost as a conversation. First, you read something, then you sit with it by taking it into your meditation – not to analyse or intellectualise it, but to allow the meaning or spirit of the words to arise from the space of meditation. Then you pray as if responding to love/

Benefits: *Provides a tool for meaning-making; offers direction and purpose; feel-good practice; leads to feelings of agency and of being guided*

Key features: *Using contemplation to expand ways of thinking*

Length: *5 to 10 minutes*

Frequency: *Daily, first thing in the morning*

Tools: *A carefully selected text, a notepad and pen; optional – cup of tea!*

Best practised: *With a text of your choice*

divine/spirit/god. Finally, you contemplate, engaging your beautiful thinking mind to consider how and where what you've uncovered might be integrated into daily life.

A delicious description of this process is offered in a book called *Soul Feast* by Marjorie Thompson, where she likens the process to 'feasting on words'. First, you take a small bite (read), then you savour the flavours and textures (meditation), then you recognise and give thanks for its essence and nourishment (pray), then you digest it (contemplate), making it part of who you are. What a beautifully subtle, slow, profound process. It serves to remind us that it is not the text, book or scripture itself that is sacred, but the essence, meaning and energy of the words themselves.

How to practise this meditation at home

To practise *Lectio Divina*, follow the four simple steps, as taught centuries ago.

Step one: Carefully select something to read as part of the practice. This could be a collection of poems, readings or a book. It might be a religious text such as the Bible. It might be a self-help book, spiritual book or even fiction such as a spiritual fantasy novel. If you're working with poetry, read one poem as part of your practice. If you have selected a book, read one section. Read your selection of text and absorb the meaning.

Step two: Take the message of what you have read into your closed-eye meditation. It doesn't need to make sense but just keep with you the essence of the text. Close your eyes, relax your body, and focus on your breathing for ten minutes.

Step three: Keep your eyes closed and stay in a meditative state but turn your focus to prayer. Ask divine energy a question, for clarification, for guidance. Ask divine energy for something. Ask divine energy to help someone or something else. Speak silently in your mind, or out loud to the divine source of energy you resonate with.

Step four: Take a deep breath and open your eyes. Take your gaze out to nature, if you can. You might like to hold a warm cup of tea or journal some thoughts into a notebook. Contemplate and reflect on what you have uncovered and how it might be lived out in your daily life.

Reflection

The American poet, Mary Oliver famously shared that she read a different poem, written by Rumi (a 13th century mystic and poet), every morning as part of her morning routine. Rumi's poetry was her source of *Lectio Divina*. I have friends who do the same with a metaphysical text *A Course In Miracles*, the Bible, the Koran or a beautiful book authored by Mark Nepo called *The Book of Awakening*. Words aren't just a source of knowledge, something that gives to us. They can be reflective mirrors or a threshold to deeper understanding about ourselves and the mysteries of the universe. Words are wisdom passed down, unlost truths that resonate on a primordial level far beneath the net of the conscious mind. Channelled words bring us closer to a sense of meaning, with ourselves and our place in the world. Words are sorcery and magic. They are sacred.

KUNDALINI MEDITATION
Awaken Your Potential

Coiled at the base of your spine, according to kundalini philosophy, is your inherent, unrealised potential and the source of divine feminine energy, Shakti. Translated as 'coiled' in Sanskrit, kundalini first appeared in the *Upanishads*, ancient sacred Hindu texts, and was considered to be 'the science of energy'. Through kundalini practices, static energy can be awakened, allowing it to activate, pierce up through the body and the seven chakras (energy centres), and be released out through the crown chakra of the head. This phenomenon is called a kundalini awakening. Those who've experienced it say you are left feeling in a state of pure bliss, coherence and a deep spiritual connection to all things. Although be warned, a kundalini awakening isn't always a pretty process. As the serpent of energy activates and moves stuck energy trapped in the body, it can sometimes be painful, the body can shake and jolt, cause huge emotional releases and sometimes even lead to a spiritual emergency. But we all know that trapped energy in the body has to go somewhere eventually, otherwise it festers and erupts in psycho-spiritual or psychosomatic symptoms, such as chronic pain or disease.

Kundalini practices involve yoga, sound, chanting, mudras, breathwork and meditation. Therefore a kundalini meditation will often involve a combination of these elements, targeting different energy centres to awaken, activate and move energy through the body. As a result, kundalini practices can be energising and dynamic, and can ultimately lead to an awakening within the body, mind and spirit.

Benefits: *Increases energy; provides balance, harmony and alignment; unblocks and releases stagnant energy; helps you get in flow*

Key features: *Using dynamic, feminine energy to help release your potential*

Length: *20 minutes*

Frequency: *Two to three times a week*

Tools: *Loose-fitting clothing*

Best practised: *In white clothing with a white cover or headscarf for your head*

An interesting study published in the *Journal of Alternative and Complementary Medicine* 2004[7] explored how the use of kundalini meditation worked effectively in the treatment of specific psychological disorders such as OCD, anxiety, intrusive thoughts and grief. Kundalini is undoubtedly a psychosomatic approach to meditation.

How to practise this meditation at home

Prepare: In a popular modernised movement of kundalini, practitioners wear white loose clothing and cover the crown of their head with a white cotton headscarf or napkin, which is thought to protect and promote energy flow. You may choose to do this or not, but one thing is for certain – loose-fitting clothing is undeniably the best clothes to wear for this meditation, so definitely opt for that!

Step one: Engage in some movement for around five minutes. This could be free movement of some sort, shaking or jumping, before settling into a seated position on the floor.

Step two: There are many kundalini breathing practices. For this meditation, try breathing deeply through both nostrils, visualising that you're breathing in energy and drawing it down the spine. Close off your left nostril with the ring and little fingers of your right hand and breathe out of your right nostril. Breathe in through your right nostril, visualising energy drawing from the crown of the head, down the spine. Hold, and switch to closing your right nostril with your thumb on the same hand, and breathe out through the left nostril. Breathe in through your left nostril, drawing energy down the spine... and continue for five minutes.

Step three: Mudras are hand gestures that create an energy circuit in the body (see the mudra meditation in the Regulate chapter). Close your thumbs and first fingers together and rest the backs of your hands on top of your knees.

Step four: Take a deep breath into the whole body and take your awareness to the third eye chakra, located in the space between your eyebrows. Sit in meditation, with your focus on the third eye and your hands in the mudra described above for ten minutes.

Close: When you are ready, anchor back into the present moment.

Reflection

For centuries, masculine energy has dominated the way Western society operates. Competition, productivity, accumulation, hierarchy, separation and patriarchal principles are what our culture is built upon. Principles that have seeped into the psyches of individuals, leading us, the collective, to behave and believe it is how we must function in order to succeed and survive. Yet it is evident that the imbalance of masculine and feminine energies is having devastating effects on just about every aspect of our reality, our mental and physical health, our sense of connection to Self and purpose, our spiritual health and the planet itself. We are exhausting ourselves and the world's natural resources all in the name of progress. Balance is required for anything to survive, and indeed thrive.

Masculine and feminine energies have nothing to do with gender, per se. They are polarised energies that are present and at play within all things in the natural world, including you. The rise of the divine feminine is not about the rise of 'women', although equality naturally manifests by default. Instead, it is about the rise of the divine feminine aspect within all of us, no matter which gender you identify with. The rise of the divine feminine, which is seeking balance with divine masculine energies, is essential for the health of the planet, and our own mental, physical and spiritual health. Perhaps, or at least here's hoping, kundalini is rising within us all.

GROUND

Nature Connection Meditations

*To surrender to nature
is to remember we are
nature. The only thing you
need to do to reconnect
is to remember that.*

The Meditations

I like to see nature meditations as permission slips to slow down, to be present and to let the natural world ground and revive you. The meditations themselves are a vehicle to bring you back to the natural world and your sense of interconnectivity. By simply placing your hands on the earth and letting her recharge you or breathing a deep lung full of air and acknowledging the reciprocal exchange with the trees. From the food we eat and the water we drink, to the stardust our bodies are made of – nature meditations help us remember we *are* nature, not separate from it.

Your healing, health, wellbeing – and your meditation practice – isn't something you have to do all by yourself or be in control of all of the time. Nature meditation practices remind you that you are not responsible for making everything happen. In fact, often the best gift a meditation practice can give you is the gift of surrender, to slow down, get quiet and go back to the very basics. It is in surrender that magic seems to happen and when the body can self-heal and self-regulate, when emotions are given permission to bubble up and pass through, where connection is not just a conceptual idea but is a full-body knowing and feeling that it is already part of who you are. To surrender to nature is to remember we are nature.

The only thing you need to do to reconnect is to remember that. Surrender, in this sense, is a psycho-spiritual yielding to or trusting in the process. It involves letting go of control and opening yourself to receptivity, to letting yourself be carried, absorbed or held. What a relief.

The meditations in this chapter will take you on a journey out into the great outdoors, where you will allow the earth, the moon, the forests and oceans to guide you back home to yourself, and a deep sense of peace that is only found within. Each meditation, in its own way, will encourage you to hand over control, to make things simple and to surrender your body, your emotions, your health and your healing to nature. To let her do the work for you. All you have to do is make time to practice and then let the magical, mystical, nourishing power of nature take care of the rest.

EARTHING MEDITATION
Recharge Yourself

When you are grounded, you feel calm, content, present and clear. There are a range of psychosomatic grounding techniques that help you ground thoughts, feelings and emotions to regain calm and presence. Arguably, all meditation practices could be considered to do this in some way. But the practice of 'earthing' or 'grounding' might just be one of the easiest. It is, quite simply, to make direct contact with the earth using your body, whether that is with your feet, hands or laying your whole body down on the earth.

Today, we often hear phrases similar to 'we are disconnected from nature in the modern world'. Since the Industrial Revolution, when human preoccupation turned towards technological advancement, resource exploitation and mass production, that disconnection has become rife. Nature itself became a commodity. The result has been an emotional, practical, physical and physiological disconnection from the earth, perceivable in just about every aspect of modern life. Very rarely does the average, busy person make physical contact with the earth, or give back to it. We walk on concrete in thick soled shoes. We microwave ultra-processed foods and we take, take, take. An earthing meditation helps us to reconnect and recharge. It is a simple, intuitive practice that results in a wide range of emotional benefits that science backs up beautifully.

You can think about it this way, perhaps you were taught to rewire a plug, shown the three wires – the live wire, the neutral wire and the earth wire. It is the earth wire that provides a protective process that ensures the system operates effectively and prevents it from overloading. The same principle can be applied to us humans. We need to 'earth', not only to operate

Benefits: *Promotes calmness and self-healing within the body; helps reduce pain; provides present-moment connection*

Key features: *Physically connecting the body with the earth*

Length: *Any*

Frequency: *Daily*

Tools: *Access to a garden, park, or any natural open space and a timer*

Best practised: *Outdoors, whatever the weather*

effectively but also to protect ourselves from overloading too. It is fascinating that physiologically, static energy in the body is literally earthed when your physical body touches the earth.

The physiological benefits of simply being in contact with the earth, every day, are astounding – reduced pain, as well as reduced inflammation and autoimmune diseases[1]. But the benefit I find the most magical and empowering is that it also promotes the self-healing response in the body.

How to practise this meditation at home

An earthing meditation brings ritual and intention to the practice of grounding – connecting your body to the earth, so you can deepen your reciprocal relationship with the earth. The bonus is, it is oh so very simple. In fact, there is nothing you need to 'do' but let the earth hold you. Let the earth do her magic, a kind of magic the body instinctively responds to.

Take yourself to a patch of earth, a garden, a park or a natural open space and try one of the following simple meditations.

Mindful barefoot walk
Set aside some time to go for a short walk. When it is safe to do so, and your feet can connect with the earth, take your shoes and socks off and set an intention to walk slowly and mindfully. This might just be in a circle around your garden, or walking on a beautiful sandy beach – it doesn't matter. What matters is connecting to the earth and a mindful intention. Start slowly, feeling the sensation of the soles of your feet connecting to the surface beneath you. Walk in silence, even if you're sharing the practice with others.

Touching the earth
Take a seat on the ground in a safe and comfortable outdoor space. Set a timer for ten minutes. Take a deep breath down to your belly and place the palms of both hands down to make contact with the earth. Close your eyes and allow your awareness to stay with the effortless flow of breath for the duration of the meditation.

Lie down
Lie down on your back in a comfortable position directly on the ground. Set a timer for ten minutes. Let the whole body relax. Close your eyes and breathe down to your belly. Consciously relax all the muscles of the body and focus on the sensations of the breath coming and going.

Reflection

Isn't it odd that most people find it strange to stumble across someone meditating alone in public? Imagine someone sitting in the middle of Bishopsgate in London meditating whilst the hustle and bustle of city life moves around them. People might likely stare, wonder if they're alright, or think they are bonkers and give them a wide berth. Isn't that odd! Odd that society has conveniently adapted itself to accommodate mental distress so subliminally, that a calm, grounded, present person is considered 'weirder' and less tolerable than a super-stressed person who charges through the streets. Children are experts in being captivated by the magic and beauty of nature. Our elders are accustomed to take a long pause on a bench, undistracted by technology, just to be. But should someone of working age be found doing those things – alarm bells ring all around that there's something up. We would all benefit from putting our feet on the earth, grounding ourselves and being present, an effortless way for the body, mind and spirit to recharge.

FULL MOON MEDITATION
Release and Let Go

The magic and sacredness of moon worship is present in most ancient cultures, who used the moon to track the months and seasons passing, giving each moon a name to reflect what was happening in the natural world – the flower moon or pink moon in spring, or the harvest moon in autumn, for example. However, moon worship goes a lot deeper than simply timekeeping. Across the world, the moon has been loaded with mythology, symbolism and ritual for millennia. Since ancient times, the moon has been associated with feminine energy and goddesses, and the sun as masculine energy, both representations of the divine. Interestingly, in contrast, aboriginal traditions and other southern hemisphere cultures consider the reverse, the moon to be masculine and the sun feminine.

A full moon meditation is practised at or around the peak of the lunar cycle in order to harness the power created at that time. The full moon is a time of heightened energy, stirring deep emotions and facilitating deep contemplation. Just as the moon affects the tides, it also has an effect on our physiology. Studies show that during a full moon, you are more likely to sleep less and wake up more[2]. Some might argue that is simply due to the light of the moon, but that doesn't explain the heightened emotions and erratic behaviour experienced during a full moon. A police officer friend of mine, who would not be considered spiritual at all, says they all know when it's a full moon due to the distinct rise in people's 'luna-tic' behaviour on those nights!

Benefits: *Helps process emotions; releases stuck energy; initiates and facilitates the process of letting go; encourages authentic expression*

Key features: *Connected to lunar energy and moon magic*

Length: *10 minutes*

Frequency: *Monthly*

Tools: *A piece of paper, a pen and a timer*

Best practised: *Outside on nights during or immediately surrounding a full moon*

Having a meditation ritual during this potent time of heightened energy, directing emotions and energy in an intentional way, can produce powerful results. Full moon meditations often involve letting go, releasing old wounds or cleaning stagnant energy and surrendering old thoughts, beliefs or patterns to the universe.

How to practise this meditation at home

Prepare: Set up a comfortable, safe space to meditate outside. If possible, allow the light of the full moon to touch your skin. Sit facing the moon and set a timer for ten minutes.

Step one: Breathe down to your belly, taking a few long, slow inhales. Keep your eyes open for a moment and notice the soft, nourishing light created by the full moon. Notice any shadows that are cast. Spend a few moments doing this before closing your eyes.

Step two: Feel into the connection between you and the moon. The cells of your body absorb that soft, kind, nourishing light. Drop your awareness down into the heart space. Imagine a full moon of soft light in the centre of the heart, imagine that light radiating out from you just as the full moon does. Imagine this is a portal for truth and expression.

Step three: Drop a question down into the heart space – what am I ready to let go of? What is holding me back from being truly, authentically me? What thought, behaviour, or habit is ready to be processed and released? What experience I am ready now to move on from? Allow whatever wants to surface – intuitive wisdom or emotions. Hand them all over to the moon. Let them surface and release.

Step four: When the timer sounds, you're ready to close your meditation. Take a deep breath into the heart, and place both hands over your heart space. Seal in any love, wisdom and self-connection you experienced. Feel into a sense of gratitude and strength for yourself, and the beautiful journey of life.

Close: Write out what came up for you on the piece of paper. List or free-hand journal what it is you are ready to let go of and bury the piece of paper in the earth. Bury what it is you wish to release, knowing it taught you a lesson about yourself, life and what you want. Let it contribute to the fertile ground of a new beginning. Thank the moon for her light and guidance.

Reflection

Letting go is a concept explored a lot in wellness, something often easier said than done. It can sometimes be packaged as a one-time only thing – do this ritual/practice/buy this course/think this way and, poof, it is done. This expectation puts pressure on you to be healed or on practices to be the 'cure', when really, it is a process. Letting go is a journey towards healing. I've certainly found that the lessons, the grief, the wisdom and the magic needs time to surface or pass through. And, of course, it is different for everyone. When it truly is time to let go, when you have fully processed something, rung the juice out of it, the effort to let go is easier. It might feel like the releasing of a helium balloon, or the placing down of heaving bags. We might even realise that the letting go happened all on its own without our conscious interference. Either way, there is no forcing these things. If we try to force ourselves to surrender, we find that this, paradoxically, requires... surrender. A full moon meditation can initiate that process, or support us in moving through the layers towards letting go.

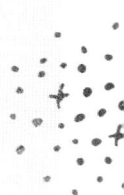

NEW MOON MEDITATION
Set Intentions

The new moon marks the beginning of a new lunar cycle and, for those who chose to live by the moon, it is the first day of a new month. The moon herself often symbolises fertility, and the new moon phase is associated with rebirth, new life and new beginnings. In the shadow, darkness and quiet, the new moon phase is like the pause between breaths, a moment of deep rest where the veil is thin, before the moon waxes and wanes, just like a deep inhale and exhale.

The grounded, introspective energy of the new moon is a potent time to set intentions, to practise manifesting, and for getting clear on what it is we want to experience. This time offers a moment to pause, time for silence and quiet contemplation before the energy of the full moon and outward expression returns. It is in meditation and quiet contemplation that we uncover our deepest desires and our truth. Nuggets of gold hidden deep in our subconscious, only accessible through ultra-presence, deep introspection, self-connection and radical honesty.

When we set intentions or goals without meditation, we might only be scratching at the surface of what is true and possible for us. What we think we want is sometimes obscured by the ego, ruled by fear or misguided self-protection. It might be a response to a current situation or affected by outside influences like family expectations or societal norms. A goal is something we work towards, a milestone or a check box that we can tick off. Setting intentions is consciously deciding on a direction of travel, to bring about an expanding feeling, an embodiment of who we truly are, rather than an accomplishment or accumulation.

Benefits: *Helps clarity and focus; offers deep rest*

Key features: *Deep introspection and connection to lunar energy and magic*

Length: *15 minutes*

Frequency: *Monthly*

Tools: *Timer, a notebook, a pen and a candle*

Best practised: *By candlelight on days during or immediately surrounding a new moon*

Setting intentions leaves room for divine surprises and magical synchronicities, and it is a foundational process that doesn't assume that we always know what is best for us. Instead, it invites us to relinquish control and to reconnect with divine guidance and support. Every month, the new moon offers us an opportunity to reflect, to realign our starting blocks in the direction of travel we want to go in, and adjust accordingly.

How to practise this meditation at home

Prepare: Take your time to set up your space. Make sure it is cosy, warm, comfortable and nourishing. Have the lights dimmed or off, and light the space you're in with candlelight. You will need to keep one candle back to light for the meditation ritual. Choose to bring in grounding aromatherapy scents such as lavender, ylang ylang or bergamot. You might choose to cleanse the space by burning incense sage or other native herbs. Have your notepad and pen to hand. Set a timer for ten minutes.

Step one: Light a candle to signify the beginning of your new moon meditation. Take a few grounding breaths, breathing down to the belly and sighing the breath out with each exhale. Feel connected to the stability and safety of the earth beneath you as you allow all the muscles in your body to relax. Notice the steadiness of your breath, the soothing rhythmical sensation of the breath rising and falling, the body being breathed by the breath. Invite a sense of space and peace to the experience.

Step two: Allow your awareness to expand upwards towards the sky, a sky only lit by sparking stars, as the new moon is hidden in the shadow of darkness. Connect with a sense of deep peace and rest. Draw your awareness back into the body but imagine the same expansion and starry night inside the body, each star a spark of unique truth, constellations of guidance formed only for you.

Step three: Connected to this expansive universe within, with infinite possibilities, drop a question into this space – what feeling do I want to experience? What feeling do I want to embody? How do I want to feel about myself? What gift can I give the world? Let any answers come. And relax back into the sense of possibility, of expansion and creativity, before the timer sounds to close your meditation.

Step four: Stay in that connected space with the candle still lit. Grab your notebook and pen and write about your experience as a stream of consciousness, allowing words to flow unedited. When your journaling comes to a natural close, take a moment to reflect on what you experienced and what came up in your journaling practice. Did some clear intentions surface? If so, take a page from your notebook and write them out. Display them somewhere you'll see them daily and reconnect to the energy behind them when you do.

Close: When you're ready to close your meditation, simply blow the candle out.

Reflection

I used to get great pleasure from setting goals each year. They were fun, motivating and rewarding. One year I set three goals – going to see a live rugby match, learning to snowboard and buying a house. I had the best night in Cardiff watching my first live rugby match, having been invited to join my dear friend Claire and her family in their box. I bought a house and I attempted to learn to snowboard (with very little success). By autumn, my goal list was ticked but I still felt empty. My life felt lacking in purpose and no matter how many fun or challenging things I added to the goals list, I would always return home to myself and all the feelings I was trying to distract myself from. It was meditation and intention setting that changed everything for me. Meditation helped me connect to my true self, and intentions allowed me to move in the direction of travel that felt authentic. The new moon is a symbol for me to check in, a reminder to get quiet, reflect and rest. The power isn't outside of ourselves to fix things, and the peace we seek isn't either. It is in you.

FOREST BATHING MEDITATION
Reduce Stress

Forests are places of mystery and magic, and in ancient cultures, trees were held as sacred. With the arrival of the Middle Ages, folklore and mythology began to portray the forest as an otherworldly realm, where fairies, spirits and danger lived. A distrust of the forest crept into the human psyche and trees were no longer held as sacred, perhaps sparking the beginning of the mass destruction of trees through deforestation. According to an article published in *Our World in Data*, 60 per cent of the world's habitable land was once covered by trees. Today, two-thirds of those trees have been lost[3].

The protection of forests was one reason that initiated a practice called *Shinrin-yoku* in Japan or 'forest bathing'. The intention of reconnecting people to the idea of the sacredness of forests, along with seeking to counterbalance the soaring levels of burnout attributed to the technological era, saw the birth of a new-old practice of being amongst the trees. *Shinrin* means forest and *yoku* means bath, and it is a mode of connection between us humans and nature.

The intimate, reciprocal relationship we have with trees never left us and will be everlasting. We breathe in the oxygen that trees breathe out, and we breathe out carbon dioxide that trees breathe in. A symbiotic relationship that nature intended. The benefits of being amongst the trees goes deeper than our respiratory system. Research has shown that trees

Benefits: *Reduces stress and anxiety; boosts the immune system; boosts mood*

Key features: *Practise mindfulness amongst trees*

Length: *Any*

Frequency: *Weekly/any*

Tools: *Quite the opposite, no tools and leave your digital devices at home*

Best practised: *In silence*

release chemicals called phytoncides, which boost the immune system. A study carried out in 2019 looked into the effects of forest bathing on people with and without a depressive tendency. It reported a significant positive effect on mental health of both groups, but specifically those with a depressive tendency[4]. Other studies have shown that forest bathing can boost mood, improve immunity and even improve attention span[5].

To practise a Shinrin-yoku inspired meditation, it requires mindfulness and forest immersion. Even the thought of that fills my body, heart and mind with relief.

How to practise this meditation at home

Prepare: Take yourself to a forest for this meditation, which will begin as you enter the forest. Turn off all electrical devices so you won't be disturbed. As you enter the forest, imagine leaving all worries and cares behind, and walk slowly and mindfully.

Step one: Practise mindfulness as you go, engaging your senses, noticing the smells, the sounds and light and shade. Find yourself a comfortable place to sit and allow your awareness to rest with your eyes for a few moments, taking in the sights of the forest. Then close your eyes. Notice the sounds, the temperature, the smells even more intimately now you're sitting down. Allow yourself to simply be present.

Step two: Take your awareness to your breath. Notice the sensation of the breath entering through the nostrils and arriving in your lungs. Breathe in with gratitude to the tree for providing such pure, clean air. As you breathe out, do so with gratitude, as if giving back to the trees. Sit with this exchange for a few minutes.

Step three: When you are ready, get up slowly and stand still for a moment, immersed in the present moment amongst the trees. Notice if you feel any subtle differences to the start of your meditation. Walk slowly and mindfully back out of the forest.

Close: As you cross the threshold back to the outside world, take note of the worries and cares you left at the edge of the forest as you walked in. Consciously decide if you want to pick them back up and examine them with a fresh, grounded perspective or whether you want to leave them behind.

Reflection

Synchronicity found me in the same tiny village in Cornwall as a friend of a friend, someone my friend had been wanting me to meet for a while because we were doing similar work in the world. We met and shared stories of our spiritual journeys, meditation and shamanism over cups of foraged nettle tea. They invited me to experience a forest meditation the next morning, led by them. I was busy writing at the time, but I couldn't remember the last time someone held space for me in that way, so I tentatively accepted.

We met as the sun was rising in wet weather coats and Wellington boots. At the mouth of the path, leading into the ancient forest hugging the banks of the River Fal, I was invited to close my eyes and trust. Easier said than done. We had only just met and now I was being led blindly into the woods! Reassured by our mutual friend connection, I closed my eyes and allowed myself to be guided by hand along the narrow winding track. After a while, they let go of my hand and invited me to follow the sound of their voice, and to trust the path in front of me. And so I did. We would stop, every now and again, and I was told to reach my hands out to blindly touch mossy tree trunks or huge leaves damp with the morning dew. After a while, I was almost striding down the path as if I had my eyes open. I could somehow see without seeing. The intensity of connection I felt to the forest around me felt transcendent, as if the guidance of my body was louder than a noise created by my mind. I remembered my inherent place amongst the trees.

MANDALA MEDITATION
Get Creative

Nature is abundant with intricate, natural mandalas, from webs painstakingly created by spiders to the geometric design of a flower in full bloom. The human relationship with mandalas dates back centuries, as far back as the Aztecs. The significance of a mandala to us humans doesn't seemed to have faded right up to modern times. They have been present in the development of numerous religious practices through to modern psychotherapy, such as that taught by Carl Jung, and even in therapies concerned with altered states of consciousness, such as holotropic breathwork founded by Stanislav Grof.

Mandala means 'sacred circle' in Sanskrit. The purpose and potency of a mandala varies, depending on which lens you are looking through. For Carl Jung, they are a representation of what he called the 'collective unconscious', a shared source of knowledge and insight amongst all things, outside of conscious awareness. He used mandalas as part of his play theory and as a tool for relaxation, helping the creator gain a deep insight into Self. In Native American cultures, the circle shape of the mandala represents the circle of life. For Buddhists, creating sand mandalas is an act of devotion and of impermanence. For Stan Grof, mandalas are an essential step in integration after a facilitated holotropic breathwork session. Within the Hindu faith, mandalas are used as a contemplative meditation aid. Either way, the creation of a mandala represents a journey or an integration, whilst reminding us of the cycle and impermanence of all things.

The creation of a mandala is a meditative act, rich in spiritual meaning, whilst offering space for reflection. You might consider that the circle symbolises unity, oneness and the cycle of life. Horizontal lines on a mandala symbolise connection to the earth and the sky. Vertical lines connect energy and represent

Benefits: *Encourages connection to nature; lowers stress and anxiety; boosts the immune system*

Key features: *Constructing a geometric shape out of natural materials*

Length: *Approximately 30 minutes*

Frequency: *Seasonally*

Tools: *Hand selected and foraged treasures found in nature*

Best practised: *On a dry day*

the connection between world, time and space. Dots are a symbol of infinite potential and possibilities. The place in which lines cross represents interconnectedness. When absorbed in the process, the creation of complex geometric shapes, and even just colouring them in, can reduce blood pressure, stress and anxiety, boost the immune system and induce meditative states. Creating a nature-based mandala is a powerful way to connect with nature at the same time.

How to practise this meditation at home

Prepare: Take yourself outdoors and set aside some sacred time to engage in your nature mandala meditation. Gather items from the natural world to create your mandala, such as stones, sticks, flowers, berries, leaves, shells, driftwood or feathers. If you are not on your own private land, ensure the items you collect have naturally fallen rather than picking flowers or leaves from trees.

Step one: Find a flat piece of earth to create your mandala upon. Settle yourself down on the ground and take a breath, centre yourself, and anchor yourself into the present moment before you begin.

Step two: Choose one item that will form the centre point of your mandala. Start by intentionally placing this, and systematically expand from there, piece by piece, layer by layer to create a symmetrical, geometric pattern.

Step three: When your mandala is complete, take a moment to enjoy your creation. You might choose to meditate on the mandala by taking a soft gaze to it whilst you connect with your breathing.

Close: When you are ready to leave, mindfully dismantle your creation. If you are in your own garden or private land, you might wish to leave the mandala in place and allow nature herself to dismantle it. If you are in a public space, it is very important to always leave no trace. Let the act of dismantling be a mindful part of the meditation.

Reflection

I bought a mandala colouring book to see what all the fuss was about. I had to buy some colouring pencils too, remembering this preference for pencils over pens from when I was young. Pens always felt too bold and final, whereas pencils felt softer and gradual. My ego voice was loud, almost poking fun at the activity as I settled down to start. 'Goodness, what would people think if they saw me now? SAD', my ego scoffed. I rolled the new, sharp pencils out of their flat box. The ritual of doing so seemed to delight some hidden part of me. I picked up the sky blue pencil and gave it a sniff – that delighted feeling intensified. And I began. Colouring and shading geometric shapes with symmetrical colour patterns, my delighted inner child was really having a ball and I seemed to get lost in it. Time stood still, yet almost an hour passed. I was in a trance-like flow state, as a sense of ease, relaxation and joy washed through me, with my inner child firmly at the helm. The only thing that would have delighted her more would have been to create a mandala in the woods, to lay it out like a gift for the fairies.

CEREMONIAL FIRE MEDITATION
Create Space

Gathering around a fire in a group of people or simply sitting by an open flame on your own, for most people feels primordial. It is almost as if our cells remember what our culture has forgotten. Fascinating research has been carried out looking into the physiological and psychological effects of sitting by a fire or watching a naked flame. A study carried out by the University of Alabama found that just watching fire lowers blood pressure, while another study published in the *Journal of Evolutionary Psychology* found that people became calmer, more sociable and more relaxed when they were gathered around a fire. This instinctual physiological response might stem from the simple fact that for our distant hunter-gatherer ancestors, being around a fire would have meant warmth, safety and belonging, and perhaps a hot meal.

In many cultures, fire ceremonies, meditations and rituals, as well as using smoke created by burning herbs and incense, are associated with purification and cleansing, and act as a bridge between the material and the eternal. Even the simple act of lighting a candle connects us to the power held within the flame. For Mac Macartney, author of *The Children's Fire – heart song of the people*, the symbolism of fire reminds us of a way of living. The book recounts Macartney's personal pilgrimage, inspired by learning of the story of children's fire. According to this Native American story, elders gathered one day to deliberate the perpetual challenge of navigating short-term needs and long-term repercussions. Once they had decided, the elders lit a fire in the middle of the circle as a symbol of a promise they would make. They proclaimed that the fire was there to remind them to never make a decision for their community that would have a negative impact on children and the generations to come. They believed

Benefits: *Releases stuck emotions; breaks energetic cords; releases and creates space for the new*

Key features: *Placing what it is you're ready to let go of on a fire*

Length: *20 minutes*

Frequency: *Monthly, ideally around the full moon*

Tools: *Access to a log burner, campfire, fire pit or just a candle, pen and paper*

Best practised: *In a group of trusted people*

securing a safe and prosperous future for their children was the most valuable investment they could make. The children's fire was a pledge to put children, future generations and nature over any seductive short-term gains. The fire became a symbol and a story passed down through generations.

Whether it is just you, sat by a fire to meditate, or if you gather around a fire with your community to pledge your own promise to future generations, or ceremonially hold space for each other and practise the meditation here, there's a mystical power infused within the fire. A connection made between the material world and the spiritual.

How to practise this meditation at home

Prepare: Safely light a fire – it could be a log burner, a campfire outdoors or a candle.

Step one: Spend a few moments noticing the movement, energy and light of the flames. Engage your senses to notice the sounds, the smells, the heat. Allow the dancing flame to draw you into a meditative state.

Step two: Pick up the paper and pen and write down what it is you would like to release and let go of. Allow yourself to deeply feel the feelings associated with what you have written down. Imagine that energy transferring into the page. Bring to mind all the lessons you learned or what gift that thing gave.

Step three: Say out loud what you are ready to release, and why. Say out loud all the things you are thankful for that that thing brought you, before gently placing the paper onto the fire. Imagine the flames cleansing and purifying the energy you release through the paper. Watch the smoke as it rises.

Close: Ensure any fire has been safely extinguished before leaving it unattended.

Reflection

Under the light of a full Hay Moon we ran, naked as the day we were born, into the ocean. Two of my oldest friends came down to visit me in Cornwall with the intention of holding a fire ceremony, to let go of the old and create space for the new. Each of us carefully selected a handful of items that we were willing to burn, including photos and old letters (one friend brought a whole bin bag full of things!). We'd each selected songs to be played whilst we were in the process. Songs that reminded us of the person, the places and the feeling we were ready to release, to really evoke any emotions held within us. We drove down to the beach, made a small campfire and held space for each other. Taking it in turns to speak out loud about what we were releasing and why, along with gratitude for what that person/place/feeling taught or gave us. Tears fell down our cheeks, crying for ourselves and for each other until the last thing turned to ash. The only sensible thing to do next was cleanse ourselves with a moonlight ocean dip!

OCEAN BREATHING MEDITATION
Calm Anxiety

A lot of people, including myself, feel magnetically drawn to water. Simply by being by the ocean, a lake or river, a sense of calm seems to wash through us. It feels like settling into ourselves. An easy, natural arrival into presence. Dr Wallace J Nichols refers to this calm meditative state as 'blue mind' in his book of the same name. His extensive research shows that just by being near water, we experience enormous health benefits, from enhanced relationships to a calmer, happier state of mind, and an improved general sense of wellbeing. One study went as far as to show that being by the ocean had comparable effects to treating depression as the use of antidepressants. After decades of research, Dr Nichols found that the brain almost immediately activates a calming response not just when you are physically near water but even when you visualise it.

An ocean meditation is a guided visualisation meditation inspired by these natural soothing, calming and healing qualities of the ocean. When paired with breathwork the benefits are amplified. It involves visualisation, activating the senses with sound, and including a breathwork practice called *ujjayi*.

Ujjayi, or 'ocean breath', is a pranayama practice in yoga. The sound created is reminiscent of the sound of waves, hence its name. This ocean sound is created by constricting the back of the throat, then breathing slowly, with extended inhales and exhales. Similar to the calming effects of being by or imagining the ocean, ujjayi breath helps to calm the mind, reduces anxiety, lowers blood pressure and slows the heart rate.

Benefits: *Boosts happiness and calmness; improves wellbeing; reduces anxiety and blood pressure*

Key features: *Being by the ocean, visualising it or breathing like the sound of the waves*

Length: *15 minutes*

Frequency: *Daily*

Tools: *Optional – recording of soothing ocean waves*

Best practised: *By the ocean*

How to practise this meditation at home

Ocean visualisation

Prepare: Press play on the recording of gentle ocean waves. Get comfortable in a restorative posture so you can completely surrender and relax. Signal to the body it is safe to relax by taking a few deep breaths, activating the parasympathetic nervous system.

Step one: Engage ujjayi breathing by constricting the back of your throat, making a wave sound as you breathe in and out. Stay here, with the breath, for a few moments.

Step two: Allow your awareness to rest on the sound of the waves and the sounds of your ujjayi breathing, and allow them to help you to visualise an ocean scene. Imagine the colour of the water, the sky and the sand. Imagine being in a comfortable position on the sand, with the sun on your skin and a gentle breeze keeping you cool.

Step three: Allow the mind drift into a trance, soothed and guided by the ocean sounds.

Close: Take a deep breath and a big stretch. Notice how you feel.

Ocean gazing meditation

Prepare: Set yourself up in a safe and comfortable seated position with the ocean in view, and the sound strongly present. You can set a timer if you wish or simply allow yourself to stay here for as long as you feel called.

Step one: Take a few rounds of breath, breathing deeply and slowly. Allow your body and mind to arrive into the present by activating your senses. Hear the sound of the waves. Notice the light, the depth and the power of the ocean. Feel the infinite possibilities of an endless horizon.

Step two: Allow your gaze to soften and rest on the waves as they come and go, alert to the sounds of the wave. Activate ujjayi breathing and feel your own breath in unison with the waves.

Step three: Let the rhythmical presence of the waves soothe the mind, body and spirit. Be at one with the ocean.

Close: Take a deep breath and a big stretch. Notice how you feel.

Reflection

I wrote a poem, one fretful day, reminding myself that 'at the depths of the ocean there is always calm, even when the waves are raging war against the skies'. I was standing in my kitchen, triggered by disappointment and gripped by anxiety. I allowed myself to be the loving observer of the experience, and those feelings seemed to have less power. How curious, that each feeling as it passes through the body seems to hold an energetic charge that ripples out like waves. Trying to tame the emotional waves requires a lot of effort with little success but connecting to the well of calm deep within me, felt soothing and powerful.

Remembering this, I took a deep breath and headed to the ocean, notebook in hand. I sat for a few minutes, breathing, listening, gazing at the deep blue sea and the endless horizon. The fret and anxiety seemed to wash away, as I scribbled down the poem – at the depths of the ocean there is always calm, just as it is within me.

FIVE ELEMENTS MEDITATION
Experience Harmony

The five elements – water, fire, air, earth and spirit/ether – embody an ancient understanding of how the natural world works. Each element is interrelated, always in motion, always transforming and influencing each other. Every living thing, including us, is influenced by these elements.

Taoism and traditional Chinese medicine (TCM) are philosophies and practices that are centred around the elements and their interplay. Their philosophies offer a basis of explanation for interconnectedness with nature and are the building blocks of all material existence. Hindus and Buddhists also hold the elements as central to their teachings and understandings. The practice of Ayurveda medicine, as well as TCM, observes the interplay of these elements within the body and mind, recognising that everything in life is created with varying proportions of these five elements.

When applying the five elements theory to the treatment of illnesses and diseases, it seeks to understand and treat the person as a whole, not just an isolated symptom. Published research in 2020 found that when Western medicine utilised the five elements theory, including TCM and homoeopathic approaches, treatment was more effective[6].

A five elements meditation adopts this whole body approach, and seeks to balance the elements within us, reconnecting us to the universal flow of nature. It might often involve bringing physical representations of each element into your practice – a candle for fire, a crystal

Benefits: *Offers feelings of unity and harmony; provides flow and grounding; invokes a sense of peace and belonging*

Key features: *Consciously connecting to the five elements – earth, water, air, fire, ether/spirit*

Length: *10 to 30 minutes*

Frequency: *Monthly*

Tools: *A crystal or stone, a feather, a candle, some water, an image of the stars or your favourite constellation*

Best practised: *First thing in the morning before dawn or in the dark of night*

for earth, sacred water from a natural stream or a glass of drinking water, a feather for air, an image of the stars or your favourite constellation for ether. It can also be practised by bringing to mind and honouring the elements within and around the human body, where we consciously connect to the earth, the breath, to passion, the blood and water within the body and space that we inhabit.

How to practise this meditation at home

Prepare: Gather any items to represent the five elements into a simple altar. Light the candle when you are ready to begin. Spend a few minutes on each of the following stages. Let them be unhurried and fully embodied.

Step one: Hold the crystal in your hand. Feel your connection to the earth through your body. Feel into the earthy quality of your bones and skeletal structure. Feel the energy within your body ground down into the earth, feel held by it.

Step two: Hold the feather in your hand. Connect to your breath. Observe the effortless flow of breath coming and going through the body, the expansion of the chest with the inhale and the gap between breaths. Connect into the sensation of air around you and the miraculous life-giving process of drawing it in through each breath.

Step three: Gaze at the flame of the candle if it feels comfortable to do so. Imagine taking the light of the flame into your heart and belly, allowing it to feed your inner passion. Feel warmth from within the body. Feel or imagine the heat and energy given to the body from the sun.

Step four: If you have a glass of water, mindfully take a sip with gratitude. Contemplate the journey of that water and the nourishment it provides you – the water of life. Alternatively, hold a jar of water in your hand and contemplate the same. Connect to the water within the body, the flow of blood and the life-giving essence of it. Expand your awareness to imagine the source of each natural spring and stream, and the rivers leading to the oceans. Contemplate the depths and vastness of the oceans, and the hidden oceans beneath the earth's crust.

Step five: Become aware of the space between your breaths, between sounds and the physical space you are in. Allow your awareness to expand to the infinite cosmos, full of stars, moons, planets and mystery. Contemplate the miracle and privilege it is to be a part of it.

Close: When you are ready, anchor yourself back into the present moment.

Reflection

Feeling rusty and unenthusiastic, I sat down to practise a five elements meditation. It was the first seated meditation I'd practised for a couple of weeks. A crazy busy schedule meant all routines were disturbed and my meditation practice had slipped out of habit. Almost dragging myself to it, I gathered my tools from a seasonal altar, and I poured myself a fresh glass of water. Begrudgingly, I started with the water. I mindfully sipped and I felt the energy of my body ground and my willingness to be in meditation increase. I closed my eyes and continued to sip. Feeling gratitude for the fresh drinking water, it reminded me of my intimate relationship with nature. I felt a visceral connection to the rivers and oceans within me as I drank. I turned my awareness to breath and air, to candle and my own sense of digestive fire, to the earthly elements of the bones within my body and my constant connection to the earth. It was as if the meditation turned me inside out. I felt refreshed and reminded of my natural essence and the privilege to be a part of it all.

NATURE SOUNDS MEDITATION
Drop into Resonance

Why does the sound of a tweeting bird on a spring day bring a sense of joy? Why does listening to the gentle flow of a stream help you ease into a state of calm? The answer comes when we investigate the measurable healing qualities within the body and mind when we listen to the sounds of nature. Nature sounds have been proven to activate the parasympathetic nervous system and be a perfect, natural antidote to overstimulation or chronic stress. But there's a deep layer of resonance that can occur too, which might often be overlooked because of the beauty of nature's glorious sounds.

The planet itself has what is known as a natural frequency – 7.82 hertz – sometimes referred to as Schumann resonance. Studies have shown that the human brain is in the optimal state of coherent wellness and health when it resonates with the earth's frequency. Research has found that this frequency was easily measurable in nature – in the forest, moors, mountain, lakes and oceans, but it is impossible to measure in built-up areas. Man-made vibrations seem to override this natural frequency. The earth's frequency is known to NASA as the earth's heartbeat and it is created by lightning in the earth's atmosphere[7]. Modern day vibrations, such as traffic, wifi and TVs, add to our stress hormones. Being in nature, immersed amongst her frequencies and sounds has the opposite effect, cortisol levels in our bodies are decreased and a greater sense of resonance is possible. If you're not able to get out in nature, listening to recordings of nature sounds can still have an effect.

Benefits: *Reduces stress; induces relaxation; boosts positivity; helps balance the mind*

Key features: *Listening to nature either outdoors or listening to a recording*

Length: *10 minutes plus*

Frequency: *Daily*

Tools: *A timer; optional – a recording of nature sounds*

Best practised: *Outdoors in nature*

It's so simple, isn't it really? Listening to nature, either out in nature or via a recording, helps reduce stress, aids relaxation and boosts positivity. Our bodies just want to be immersed in nature, their original home. There's nothing we need to 'do' to encourage cortisol levels to drop. If we allow it, nature will do that for us. All we need to do is make the time to practise and hand over the healing powers to nature.

How to practise this meditation at home

Prepare: Choose a time and day that will allow you to be outside for this meditation. If it is impossible for you to get to a natural space, you can find a recording of nature sounds and listen to it for the duration of your meditation.

Step one: Set ten to fifteen minutes aside for this meditation. You can set an alarm on your phone if you need to but if you can, turn your phone off or onto airplane mode. Take out your earbuds and take off your smart watch. Allow yourself to be undisturbed by technology during this meditation.

Step two: Settle into a posture that you can keep for the duration of your meditation. This could be seated, lying down or standing. As you allow the body to settle into stillness, engage the sense of sight. Really notice the detail of the space you are in before closing your eyes. Now take your full focus and awareness to your ears. Notice the interplay of sounds around you. Notice sounds that are close by and those that are in the far distance. Notice any space between sounds.

Step three: Let go of any effort to hear sounds and instead see if you can relax into the orchestra of sound of the present moment. Let the sounds wash through you, sooth you and heal you. Let it all happen by itself with no effort or control. Allow the mind to drift and dream. If any images or memories bubble up from your subconscious, allow them to.

Close: When the timer sounds or you feel it is time to come out of your meditation, take some time to anchor back into the present moment by engaging all senses. Bring your awareness to your eyes once more, take a few deep breaths, notice any physical sensations in or around the body. Notice how you feel before slowly getting up and on with your day.

Reflection

During the stillness of the coronavirus lockdowns of early 2020 in the UK, it seemed to a lot of people, including myself, that the sounds of nature had gotten louder. Birds, especially, were claimed to be heard singing more loudly than usual, especially in urban gardens. But was nature really louder? Or was it simply that the humdrum of modern human activity that drowns out the sounds of the natural world was hushed, and instead we slowed down enough to be able to listen more? According to the Natural History Museum[8] seismologists measured a 50 per cent drop in vibrations during lockdown due to the decrease in noisy human activity. A study carried out in 2021[9] looked at how gardens functioned as a therapeutic landscape during the pandemic, citing the report that birds felt louder due to a greater attunement by people to nature.

Nature sounds are always there, however subtle, whether it's a gentle brush of the breeze through the trees, the sounds of falling rain, water flowing or those magical birds tweeting. When we pause to tune into it, an instant calming, mood-boosting effect can be experienced, as if breaking us out of the monotony of mental chatter, anchoring us back into a sense of peace and harmony. Somewhere deep in us is reminded of what we are a part of, and what a beautiful planet this is.

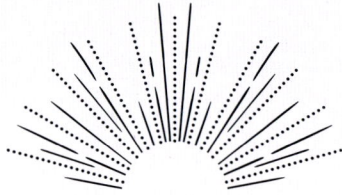

REGULATE

Mind-Body-Spirit Meditations

'Self' experience is influenced by and interconnected to nature, energy, vibration and collective forces outside of the Self and conscious human awareness. This is a whole-person approach.

The Meditations

Throughout this chapter, you will find some super simple practices that will help you facilitate an inner sense of interconnection between mind, body and spirit. They will help regulate your nervous system, calm your mind, attune to your own sense of spiritual connection and protection, and align all aspects of your whole and beautiful self. I hope they will help you to find safety and flow in the present moment and a sense of calm and harmony from within.

The mind-body connection is undeniable, and an increasing body of research is proving just how powerful and intertwined this connection really is. At its core, the mind-body connection is a psychosomatic feedback loop where our thoughts, emotions, beliefs and attitudes have an impact on our physiology and vice versa. The food we eat, and how we hold, move or treat our bodies have an impact on our mental state, health and wellbeing. The mind and the body are not two separate entities, as Western medicine has believed since the early 18th century, but instead the mind and the body are intrinsically interlinked, inseparable from each other. This approach is often referred to as a whole-person approach.

The mind-body-spirit connection goes one step further, and is more aligned with the whole-person approach upheld in ancient teachings. This is also one central theme for an emerging school of psychology called Transpersonal (or holistic) psychology. This school of thought acknowledges and values the 'other than human' influences on our health, wellbeing and the human experience, just as much as our mental and physical health. It recognises and values that the 'Self' experience is also influenced by and interconnected to nature, energy, vibration and collective forces outside of the Self and conscious human awareness. This approach truly is whole person. As the saying goes, 'we are spiritual beings having a human experience'.

Mind-body-spirit meditations value these three interconnected aspects – the miraculous physical body, mind and spirit. When these three aspects are in harmony and regulated, we experience harmony and regulation. Aligning and anchoring the mind, body and spirit in the present moment through meditation is one simple way we can attend to the inner and outer experience of regulation.

HEART CENTRE MEDITATION
Experience Coherence

Most of us have heard of the body-mind connection. But there's one connective relationship that doesn't get quite as much air-time: the heart-brain connection. The heart-brain connection is the centre of focus of an organisation called the HeartMath Institute. Their extensive research has demonstrated that the heart and the brain are in constant reciprocal communication, known as coherence[1]. Emotional states linked to different heart activity have curious effects on our cognitive processes. One of the most significant contributors to heart rate variation is our emotions or feelings. How fascinating to consider that our emotions can not only manifest in the body perhaps as a smile, tears or an ache of pain, but the beat and vibration of our heart are altered too.

The spiritual significance of the heart has long been acknowledged in ancient teachings concerning meditation. The heart centre is said to be a vibrational or electromagnetic field surrounding the heart. In the ancient Ayurvedic text *Upanishads*, the heart centre was considered to be a sort of spiritual portal or a 'self-luminous consciousness' – meaning that it can omit its own light and energy. I love the phrase 'the portal of the heart' and find myself saying it often in my own teachings. Could it be a portal to a higher state of consciousness? Could it be a portal to healing, integration or coherence? Is it a portal to the divine? For some, this portal is where we can access wisdom and guidance from the unified field or collective consciousness. Others consider that when the heart, mind and body are in coherence, a greater state of wellbeing can be experienced.

Benefits: *Helps emotional stability and making effective decisions; accesses positive emotions*

Key features: *Bringing your awareness consciously into the heart space*

Length: *10 minutes*

Frequency: *Daily*

Tools: *Timer and a candle; optional – blanket, essential oils and music*

Best practised: *First thing in the morning and/or last thing at night*

Some spiritual traditions suggest that we see through the eye of the heart. What is fascinating is that the heart sends more information to the brain than the brain does to the heart. It even has its own micro-nervous system and is considered to be precognitive, a term meaning having foresight before an event actually happens – otherwise known as intuition. Meditating on the heart space can activate the passage of communication to our brain and our whole body, creating coherence and activating a portal to intuition. What magic.

How to practise this meditation at home

This practice is one of my personal favourites. A deeply 'yin' practice, this meditation is all about love, comfort and kindness.

Prepare: Sit or lie down in a posture that feels really nourishing and comforting. No rules, instead listen to your own body, mind and heart and let that guide the posture you choose. You might like to wrap a blanket around your shoulders or over your legs or cradle a hot water bottle. Set a timer for 10 minutes, or however long you have.

Step one: You might choose to listen to some soothing meditation music. Search 'Meditation Music – Joey Hulin' on Spotify and you'll find a playlist of some of my favourites. You might also choose to bring essential oils into the practice. Rose, lavender or ylang-ylang are nurturing scents that can arouse feelings of love and support from the heart chakra. Take a few gentle breaths of the essential oil, or rub a few drops of skin-safe oil onto the pulse points of the wrist, neck or the centre of the breastplate.

Step two: Light your candle to signify the beginning of your meditation.

Step three: Close your eyes and allow your awareness to drop down into the heart space. Notice the weather of the heart, without judgement. Take a few long, slow deep breaths, imagining the breath gathering up that energetic weather, and clear it with the outbreath, allowing you to access your heart more deeply. Notice the energy of the heart – does it feel open and plump? Does it feel tight and closed like a bud of a flower? Direct every gentle easy breath to the heart space. Imagine the breath easing any tension, softening any tightness and allowing that bud to softly open.

Step four: Imagine a light right in the centre of the heart. The light of unconditional love and pure consciousness. A space where we are all the same. Where we are connected to everything – every being, every plant, the earth and the stars. A portal of love.

Step five: Rest your awareness on the warmth and light of the heart space and the connection to unconditional love. Every breath is guiding you back home to the heart and deeper into love.

Close: When the timer sounds, place both hands over your heart space, in a loving gesture to yourself. Smile. Open your eyes and blow the candle out.

Reflection

Namaste is a word that gets tossed around in wellbeing circles so flippantly that the true meaning is lost in insincerity. I remember thinking it was just something you say at the end of a yoga practice. An exchange between teacher and students as an alternative to 'right you lot, that's it, class is done' and 'thanks for that!'. It was a brightly coloured homemade sign on the side of a dusty street in Bali that taught me the true meaning for the first time – the light in me honours the light in you. When said authentically with intention and reverence, I wonder, could there be a more beautiful thing to say to another being?

BODY SCAN MEDITATION
Relax and Unwind

A body scan meditation is a basic mindfulness practice that arose from Vipassana meditation and draws similarities with ancient Burmese traditions. A body scan, systematically scanning the body from top to bottom or bottom to top, has a deeply relaxing effect on the body. It helps elicit what Herbert Benson described as 'the relaxation response' in activating the parasympathetic nervous system, in his book *The Relaxation Response*. However, the benefits of a body scan go a lot deeper than just relaxation. It can reveal a lot about your life, your thoughts and your emotional state. A body scan meditation is about being in and listening to the body, which holds so much wisdom and truth.

As we've discussed, the mind-body connection is a constant feedback loop of information. A body scan helps to consciously identify what stories the body is trying to communicate. There is an ever-present link between emotions and physical sensations, and likewise, physical sensations are tied to emotional states. An obvious example would be when you feel nervous about something and you feel butterflies in your stomach, your heart pounds and your mouth dries up. But what about the more subtle cues, when you get a gut feeling about something or when your heart feels tender or closed – what is the body saying? What subtle emotions might be present? If you have trouble sleeping, pay attention to what is going on in the body, perhaps you'll find gritted teeth and tight fists, indicating the fight or flight response is still engaged even during sleep. Relaxing the body relaxes the mind and vice versa. And this is precisely what a body scan helps us do.

Benefits: *Helps regulate the nervous system; promotes calmness; reduces anxiety; improves sleep*

Key features: *Practical and accessible*

Length: *5 to 10 minutes*

Frequency: *Daily*

Tools: *None*

Best practised: *Can be practised anywhere at any time but it is best practised lying down*

It can be challenging to 'be in the body' for a lot of people because we, as a society, have become so disconnected from our bodies, we abuse or numb them in a multitude of different ways. It can be especially challenging to be in the body if you've experienced trauma, so please go gently if this is you. A body scan meditation helps us to stay present in the body with kindness and compassion, and allows an integration of intuitive wisdom achieved through mind-body-spirit connection to naturally arise.

How to practise this meditation at home

Prepare: The intention of this practice is to simply notice what is there in the body and consciously relax any tension. It doesn't matter if you're lying down, seated, standing or even moving through your daily doings. However, for this practice, you might like to lie down and get as comfortable as possible.

Step one: Begin by taking a deep breath. Practice mindfulness and anchor yourself in the present moment. Close your eyes.

Step two: Start at the top of the head and imagine your awareness melting down over your forehead. Notice if there is any tension in the muscles of the face, between the eyebrows, around the eyes and the jaw. Consciously soften and relax any tension you find.

Step three: Allow your awareness to melt down through the neck, the shoulder and down the arms. Allow this intention of relaxation to move with it.

Step four: Continue, slowly, down through the whole body to the tips of the toes. Allow the whole of your body to relax.

Step five: Stay here for a few minutes and notice if any tension creeps back in. If it does, soften and relax once more.

Close: Take a deep breath and open your eyes.

Reflection

Herbert Benson, an academic researcher, spent time in India in the 1970s experiencing yoga and meditation for the first time. On his return home to the States, he was surprised how different he felt. Being a scientist, he had to understand why.

He carried out a study comparing the stress response of people in three groups – non-meditators, new meditators and seasoned meditators. He exposed each group to a series of stressors and measured their physiological response. When under stress, the responses we might all recognise kicked in – heart rate increased, palms sweated, breath quickened. No surprises there. But it was what happened in the gaps between stressors that he was interested in. The study found that once the stressor had ceased, the group of experienced meditators appeared to come back down to a baseline level of physiological regulation much quicker than the other two groups. But the crucial finding was that some participants in the group of non-meditators didn't come back to a baseline level between stressors at all. They stayed in a heightened state of stress throughout the whole of the experiment.

Reflecting on my own experience as a non-meditator, I knew that feeling all too well. Experiencing a lingering feeling of anxiety running in the background of all daily experiences, and a continuous string of sleepless nights, so much so that insomnia became my norm. A simple, uncomplicated meditation practice, such as a body scan, can help us navigate our way back to that regulated baseline level, back to calm. It might seem basic but with consistent practice, it can be life changing.

CHAKRA MEDITATION
Find Balance

According to ancient Vedic philosophy, there are seven energy centres in the body, known as chakras. The chakras (meaning 'wheel' or 'disc' in Sanskrit) move through levels of consciousness, from the very basic human need to survive at the root, right up to universal connection and oneness at the crown of the head. Briefly, the seven chakras are:

The root chakra (*Muladhara*) at the base of the spine. When in balance, you'll feel grounded and safe with a strong sense of social and family belonging. When out of balance, you might have issues with money, housing, feeling safe and secure.

The sacral chakra (*Svadhisthana*) just below the belly button. When in balance, you'll feel creative, powerful, able to take calculated risks, and able to express your emotions. When out of balance you might find it difficult to express joy, play or enjoy a healthy sex life.

The solar plexus chakra (*Manipura*) just above the belly button, below the ribs. When in balance, you'll feel confident and capable, with a strong sense of who you are and a connection to your instinct. When out of balance, you might feel powerless, ruled by fear of criticism or by a very loud inner voice of criticism.

The heart chakra (*Anahata*) in the heart and chest cavity. When in balance, you'll feel joy, gratitude and compassion for yourself and others. When out of balance, you might feel closed, bitter, jealous or lonely.

The throat chakra (*Vishuddha*) in the throat. When in balance, you can express yourself easily and creatively. You are honest and truthful. When out of balance, you might struggle to express yourself, feel disconnected or out of control.

Benefits: *Helps with psycho-physiological connection, balance and self-awareness; unblocks stuck energy; helps mind-body-spirit balance*

Key features: *Visualising and connecting with the seven energy centres in the body*

Length: *10 to 15 minutes*

Frequency: *Weekly*

Tools: *None*

Best practised: *Consistently over a period of time*

The third eye chakra (*Ajna*) in the space just between your eyebrows. When in balance, you can see things clearly, and have a strong sense of trust, insight and divine connection. When out of balance, you might feel out of touch with reality and unable to look at what is really happening or there in front of you.

The crown chakra (*Sahasrara*) at the very top of your head. When in balance, you are able to live fully in the present moment with balance, ease, trust and harmony. You are spiritually awake and conscious. When out of balance, you might feel overly identified with the ego, power or self-importance. You might feel confused or be stuck in your ways.

How to practise this meditation at home

This chakra meditation involves systematically moving your awareness through each energy centre, allowing energy to flow and mind-body-spirit balance to be regained.

Prepare: In a comfortable position, close your eyes and move through each chakra, breathing life into each energy centre, imagining the breath shifting and moving any stuck energy.

Step one: Take your awareness to the root chakra. Imagine a spinning disc of red light. Repeat the affirmation 'I am safe. I am home. I am welcome. I am loved'.

Step two: Take your awareness to the sacral chakra. Imagine a spinning disc of orange light. Repeat the affirmation 'I am creative. I allow myself pleasure. I validate my emotions and needs. I allow myself to receive'.

Step three: Take your awareness to your solar plexus. Imagine a spinning disc of yellow light. Repeat the affirmation 'I enjoy life. I am strong and capable. It is safe to be me'.

Step four: Take your awareness to your heart chakra. Imagine a spinning disc of green or pink light. Repeat the following affirmation 'I am loved. I am grateful. I forgive myself and others. I am whole'.

Step five: Take your awareness to your throat chakra. Imagine a spinning disc of blue light. Repeat the following affirmation 'I express myself easily. I communicate truthfully. I am connected, creative and authentic'.

Step six: Take your awareness to your third eye chakra. Imagine a spinning disc of purple light. Repeat the following affirmation 'I see things clearly. I trust my insight. I am divinely guided. I trust life'.

Step seven: Take your awareness to your crown chakra. Imagine a spinning disc of violet or white light. Repeat the following affirmation 'I am whole. I am at peace. I trust the universe. I am connected'.

Close: Bring to mind all seven chakras, in perfect alignment. As you breathe in, imagine breathing up from the root chakra right through to the crown, then back down, as you breathe out. Stay here for as long as you need. When you are ready to close, take a long, slow deep breath and place your hands over your heart before opening your eyes.

Reflection

Whether you believe in energy centres or not, a chakra meditation can facilitate self-reflection, helping you identify areas in your life where you might feel a little stuck. I find it fascinating that for me and a lot of class attendees over the years, it is easier to visualise some colours during a chakra meditation than others. And on reflection, the colours that are harder to see do always seem to correlate to the areas of life or Self that feel blocked. I can even trace a link between physical illnesses I've experienced and an energetic block in my own chakra system. A chakra meditation gives us a map for deeper exploration. Consciously bringing awareness to all seven energy centres can create a sense of harmony and balance through the body, the mind and the spirit. Bliss.

BREATHWORK MEDITATION
Feel Energised

Breathwork is a multi-discipline practice that has been around for millennia. It essentially involves the intentional use of the breath to induce meditation or physiological benefits. There are numerous approaches to breathwork, and it has undoubtedly become a wellbeing trend in the modern day. Some practices are attributed to Vedic and yogic practices of pranayama. In more recent times, Stanlav Grof, a scientist researching altered state of consciousness, developed the holotropic breathwork approach. Holotropic breathwork is a form of induced hyperventilation in a safe, controlled, ceremonial setting undertaken intentionally to release past or hidden trauma. The Wim Hof breathing technique, undoubtedly a current wellbeing trend, also involves inducing a form of hyperventilation similar to holotropic breathwork. Breathwork approaches range from altered states of consciousness to the very simple 'one conscious breath is a meditation' but all breathwork seems to have an incredible effect on the mind-body connection.

One study investigated the effects of simply slowing down the breathing, as a form of breathwork practice, and found these very basic practices increased comfort, relaxation, pleasantness, vigour and alertness, and reduced symptoms of overexcitement, anxiety, depression, anger and confusion[2]. Breathwork could be practised for the psycho-physiological changes it seems to facilitate in the mind-body connection. But it is fascinating to think something as simple as breath control can also act as a threshold to access, process and integrate trauma and experiences hidden in the depths of our unconscious mind, but which continue to present themselves in physical or psychological ways.

We are often told to 'be present' but for some who have experienced trauma by simply becoming present, this can exacerbate the feelings they are trying so hard to mask, numb or avoid. The present moment just reveals to us what is there, things that might need facing, such as unresolved trauma or challenging emotions. Breathwork can be a particularly useful tool for those who find it hard to practise mindfulness, because it regulates the nervous systems and helps the body relearn that it is safe in the present moment. It brings about the body's natural relaxation response as well as activating the parasympathetic nervous system.

Benefits: *Helps regulate the nervous system; increases energy; encourages being in the present*

Key features: *Intentionally controlled or restricted breathing techniques*

Length: *Try starting with 5 minutes and work your way up*

Frequency: *Daily*

Tools: *Timer*

Best practised: *In the morning*

How to practise this meditation at home

There are so many breathwork practices, too many to list, but here are three of the simplest that you can easily practise at home. If you feel light-headed during any of the practices, take a few easy breaths in between a deep breath. Or if any technique seems to exacerbate feelings of anxiety, just release the practice and breathe easy for a while.

Prepare

Set yourself up by settling into a seated position, either on the floor or on a chair. You might like to stretch, shake your hands out, or anything that would help you settle into meditation.

Set a timer for five minutes. Close your eyes and begin one of the breathing practices below until the timer sounds. Once it does, release the breathing practice and sit for a few moments in silence with your eyes closed before ending your meditation.

Deep belly breath

By engaging the abdomen, you experience the full capacity of breath. This stimulates the vagus nerve, communicating to your whole body and your mind that it is safe to relax. Let your breath be slow, not too forced or too deep, but instead breath gently and slowly down to the belly, expanding the belly with breath. It should feel easy and calming, not exaggerated, although you might find an even deeper breath or a sigh comes naturally as your parasympathetic nervous system is activated. You can release the breath with an open or a closed mouth, whatever feels best for you.

Box breathing

Breathe in through your nose for four counts. Hold for four counts. Breathe out through your mouth for four counts. Hold for four counts. Repeat.

4-7-8 Technique

Breathe in through your nose for the count of four. Hold for the count of seven. Release slowly for the count of eight through your nose or mouth, whichever feels best for you.

Reflection

Sat on the floor of a yoga studio with crossed legs, in a circle with twenty other students all mid-way through a brilliant yoga teacher training foundation course run by Devon School of Yoga, we were introduced to breath work – pranayama. With closed eyes, we began to practise the 4-7-8 technique. Breathe in for four, hold for seven, and breathe out for eight. It was only a few minutes into the practice and the room started spinning. A feeling of anxiety had charged through my experience, taking a firm hold of my body and mind. Panic started to rise. I kept my eyes closed but released the practice, allowing my breath to find its natural pace once more. While most of my fellow students experienced a deep sense of calm, riding high from a feeling of bliss afterwards, I had experienced the opposite. I had a quiet word with the teacher afterwards, who reassured me of how common it is. With the constant feedback loop of body and mind, restricted breathing causes feelings of anxiety, and anxiety causes disruption in our breathing. It's also to do with oxygen and carbon dioxide levels changing in the body. He suggested ensuring I remember to breathe down to the belly, rather breathing high up in my chest. He suggested reducing the time for each hold, 3-5-7 perhaps, and he suggested to do so gently, not with rigour or force. Settling down for our next breathing practice, my experience completely changed.

YOGA NIDRA MEDITATION
Experience Deep Rest

There is a sweet spot in all meditation practices between wakefulness and sleep. It takes practice to trust ourselves to go into that space and to stay there without falling asleep, or our nervous system jolting us back into action. In an overworked, over-stressed society, deeply in need of rest, it is no wonder so many people doze off straight away in meditation practices – our bodies and minds are calling out for deep rest. Yoga nidra gives us a name for this state of consciousness – in a deep state of rest yet not asleep.

Yoga nidra, also known as yogic sleep, is a practice that induces a deep state of relaxation, stemming from ancient tantric practices of *Nyasa*, which translates as 'to take the mind to a point'. In order to understand the benefits of yoga nidra, we turn our focus to brain wave states (see Deep Rest meditation later in the chapter). In a true state of deep rest, you will access a delta brain wave state, which is the deepest sleep cycle and the state where healing and repair can take place. In this deeper state of relaxation, the pineal gland is activated, releasing melatonin, which is a potent antioxidant and can help manage immune function, and blood pressure and balance the stress hormone cortisol[3].

The practice involves the rotation of consciousness around the body, naming each part in turn, until your awareness is held on the whole body. Intention setting, breathing and relaxing into conscious awareness are important stages of a practice. It is claimed that the technique of naming each body part was initiated by a yogi called Swami Satyananda in the 1950s, which was the birth of the practice as we know it today.

Benefits: *Promotes deep rest and relaxation; aids physiological healing that occurs during deep rest*

Key features: *Rotation of consciousness around the body*

Length: *20 minutes plus*

Frequency: *Any but weekly is good*

Tools: *A cosy blanket, low lighting, an eye mask and a timer*

Best practised: *Listening to a teacher or a guided audio track*

How to practise this meditation at home

Prepare: Set your timer for as long as you can spare. Set an intention for your practice before you begin. Get into a comfortable position, laying out flat in the yoga posture *savasana* – on your back, arms slightly away from your body, hands facing down, legs slightly apart. You might wish to cover yourself with a blanket. Close your eyes.

Step one: Starting with the thumb on the right hand, rotate your consciousness to each body part in turn – each finger, the palm of the hand, the back of the hand, the wrists, etc. Cover the whole right side of the body. Then move to the left.

Step two: Once you have rotated your awareness around the whole body, allow the whole body to relax. Allow the body to be heavy and at ease.

Step three: Notice the movement of breath throughout the body, noticing the sensations of the body breathing all by itself.

Step four: Relax into the ease of deep rest, allow the mind and body to be at ease.

Close: When the timer chimes to end your meditation, take a deep breath into the whole body. Wiggle your fingers and toes. Take a full body stretch. Find your way to a seated position and it might feel nice to rest your hands in prayer pose at your heart centre to close your practice with a smile.

Reflection

I've always had an aversion to any narrative that claims that one meditation approach is 'better' than another. I've found that this narrative pops up often in the yoga community when it comes to yoga nidra, loud voices claiming that it is better/more effective/somehow more superior to other forms of meditation. The deeper I investigate and practise various approaches to meditation, the more I've come to recognise, curiously, that this narrative is usually loudest when the technique has been developed in recent years or it is attributed or trademarked to one particular teacher. This is not to say that yoga nidra isn't powerful, it is. It's truly wonderful! But it is just one powerful technique in a chocolate box of lots of techniques.

Someone in class once asked me what the difference between yoga nidra and a body scan is, and the answer is – subtle differences. With yoga nidra, you are guided by naming body parts as you rotate consciousness around the body, whereas with a body scan you consciously relax different body parts systematically, from top to bottom or vice versa. The intention of a body scan might be mindfulness and relaxation, whereas the intention of yoga nidra might be to access the meditative state between wakefulness and sleep to aid relaxation.

SOUND HEALING MEDITATION
Re-calibrate Emotions

Sound healing is a booming practice that appears to have captured the hearts and minds of many in the Western world. It involves being given permission to completely relax and surrender for an hour or so whilst a trained sound healing practitioner plays an array of instruments. These instruments are, most commonly, crystal bowls, gongs, Koshi chimes, drums, singing bowls and tuning forks.

Sound meditations are mostly concerned with vibrations and their healing power. Quantum physics suggests that everything in the universe is energy, from the cells in your body to the natural world around us, and energy is just vibrations. Vibration is linked to brain wave states, which are an important aspect of most meditation practices. Sound practitioners claim that simply by receiving the sounds created by the instruments, the mind is guided naturally to slow down and surrender into deeper brain wave states. A natural, effortless meditative state then occurs. The mind is allowed to drift and dream during a sound meditation and there is no need to actively listen or pay attention to anything at all. Instead, you are given permission to relax and let go. It's a type of permission that is not often given in the busy culture we're a part of, nor even in a number of meditation approaches. There is nothing you need to do, fix, heal or change, other than to simply let go.

Benefits: *Reduces stress and anxiety; improves sleep; reduces pain*

Key features: *Listening to sound frequencies created by instruments*

Length: *Facilitated classes usually last 1 to 2 hours*

Frequency: *Monthly*

Tools: *You will need to attend a class or listen to an audio recording, eye pillow, blankets*

Best practised: *In a class led by a trained practitioner*

Practitioners work with six predominant frequencies of sound: 396, 417, 528, 639, 741 and 852 hertz. These are believed to bring about a sense of harmonised emotional wellbeing, activate DNA repair and can even ease physical pain. Research shows that they can induce altered states of consciousness and reduce anxiety and chronic stress[4]. What is interesting to note is, it is a practice that is also claimed to be able to stir and trigger dormant emotions trapped in the body. Sometimes this can be challenging to sit with, but releasing stuck emotions is an important step in any healing journey. Mostly, people experience a trance-like state of bliss, while others might even tip over and drift off into sleep.

How to practise this meditation at home

Attend a class

The best way to enjoy a sound healing meditation is to attend an organised event or class. They are so popular these days, I am sure if you googled your nearest practitioner, they wouldn't be too far away. My top tip is to dress super comfortably; think PJs or your comfiest jogging bottoms, and bring with you your own pillow and your favourite blankets, one to go underneath you and one to go on top. I've even seen someone bring their son's Spiderman single duvet into a sound meditation session with them. Some practitioners provide different aids to help you relax, such as eye pillows and blankets, but I always like to bring my own just in case or to double up.

Listen to a recording

If you can't get to a class, you can listen to a recording and still benefit from the healing vibrations. Spend a bit of time before you're ready to practise this meditation finding a track you enjoy. You can search online or look for a brilliant, free meditation app called Insight Timer for a quality recording that is the length and style that's just right for you.

Set up a comfy little cocoon for yourself, press play, place an eye pillow over your eyes and kick back, soaking up the healing vibrations. Allow your mind to drift and dream. Allow images and visions to come and go as you drop down into deeper meditative brain wave states.

Play an instrument at home

You can bring sound into all or any of your daily meditation practices by purchasing one quality item. This might be a Koshi chime or a Tibetan singing bowl. The vibration and sounds of both help initiate a meditative state and can be a pleasant and ritualistic way to start or end any meditation practice. Even taking one minute to just play the instrument can help you come home to yourself and the present moment in an easy, enjoyable way.

Reflection

I was slap-bang in the middle of a particularly busy week. It felt as if a cold was brewing and I was exhausted. A dear friend of mine invited me to join her for a Yin Yoga and Sound Bath class that Friday night. I eagerly accepted. I'd been to many sound baths before, from ones where they had too many instruments to count – flutes, chimes, drums, didgeridoos, literally all the bells and whistles – to more modest sound baths with a few simple chimes and crystal bowls. All sound experiences had been divine. We arrived late and squeezed into a spot at the back of the hall near the door. We practised some yoga before settling down for the sound meditation.

The gong hammering began. Dong, dong, dong, dong, she bashed away at the giant gong at the front of the hall. Seconds in I felt agitated. Ten minutes in and I was ready to explode with rage. I was fascinated to witness the agitation and frustration the aggressive gong banging was bringing up in me. I curled over onto my side into a foetal position and tried to focus on my breathing. 'It'll be over soon' I thought to myself. Sound has the power to stir all sorts of emotions in us, including those trapped or locked away. I rarely let myself experience agitation or anger in daily life. The experience in the sound meditation made me realise that there was plenty there within me, whether I consciously faced it or not.

MUDRA MEDITATION
Circulate Energy

The main intention of practising a mudra meditation is to allow a flow of life-force energy to move through the whole body, energy known in a number of Eastern traditions as *prana*. By touching fingers and thumbs together, in a meaningful way, facilitates a quieting of the mind, allowing a deep state of meditation to be accessed. Mudra translates from Sanskrit as 'gesture' or 'seal' and the practice means to form a symbolic shape with the hands, often with certain fingers or thumbs touching. Mudras are used in spiritual practices to balance the five elements within the body, to unblock stuck energy and to create a universal flow of energy through and around the body. The fingers create an energetic circuit for prana to flow and each finger correlates to one of the five elements. Mudra can often be paired with breathing exercises or practices alongside chanting a mantra too. There are hundreds of mudras, some involving more than just the hands but most use a very simple gesture such as closing the index finger to the thumb. This mudra is known as the *gyan mudra* or *chin mudra*, which is said to aid concentration and focus, boost positivity and help connect us to our higher self.

An interesting study carried out in 2022 looked at the effects of mudra meditation paired with breathwork on immunity. This small study suggests that improvements to health, wellbeing and immunity can be found through a mudra practice[5]. Another study involving hypertensive Indian paramilitary personnel found a significant reduction in stress among participants who again paired mudra meditation with breathing techniques[6].

Benefits: *Lowers anxiety; promotes grounding and focus; encourages self and divine connection*

Key features: *Holding simple hand gestures involving fingers and thumbs during meditation*

Length: *10 minutes*

Frequency: *Daily*

Tools: *A candle*

Best practised: *Paired with breathing techniques or mantras*

Holding a mudra during meditation can also act as an anchoring technique for anxiety. When you close a finger and thumb together and enter a deep state of meditation and relaxation, your body-mind connection will make an association between the two things. Then, in moments of stress or anxiety in everyday life, practising that same mudra can help anchor us into a felt sense of safety and break any feelings of being overwhelmed.

How to practise this meditation at home

The meditation framework

Here are three very simple mudras for you to try out at home. Your practice will look the same for all three, just with a different mudra. Light a candle at the beginning of your meditation. Sit in a cross-legged position or sit on a chair with your feet flat on the floor. Adopt one of the mudras below and hold this hand position for the duration of your meditation. Close your eyes and take a deep breath. Notice the sensations of each breath moving through the nostrils and down the throat. Notice the sensation of the chest expanding and contracting. Notice the subtle sound of the effortless flow of breath. Allow your awareness to rest on the pause between the out breath and the next inhale. When you are ready to finish your meditation, take a deep breath and release the mudra. It might feel nice to rub the face or stretch before you blow the candle out.

Gyan mudra

Close the index finger and thumb together on both hands. Rest the back of the hands on your knees so the arms, wrists and hands are relaxed. This simple mudra is good for concentration and grounding.

Anjali mudra

Place the palm of both hands together in front of your chest, in a prayer pose with the finger pointing up towards the sky. Ensure both thumbs are pressed together. Bring the thumbs to rest on the sternum in the centre of the chest or the centre of the heart chakra. This mudra is good for a sense of self-love and acceptance.

Hunya mudra

Straighten all four fingers on both hands, then bend the middle fingers down as if they are reaching for the palms of your hands. Close your thumbs over the top of the bent fingers, keeping the remaining three fingers straight. With the palms facing up, place the backs of the hand on your knees. This mudra is good for a sense of tranquillity.

Reflection

Sat on an almost empty London underground tube making my way towards Richmond to take part in my first ever high profile podcast interview, I was feeling nervous. To make it even more intimidating, the interview was being filmed. If you ever want to see me squirm, put a camera in front of me! Whether it's having my picture taken or being filmed, it is not my comfort zone. I had made a promise to myself before I left the hotel that morning that I was going to savour and enjoy every second of the experience. It felt like a once in a lifetime opportunity that I had fortuitously been granted. It didn't feel like a step up, it felt like a quantum leap up, and the gravitas of the occasion allowed old insecurities to resurface and attempt to sabotage the earlier promise I made to myself. Sat on the tube, rattling along, I closed my eyes, pressed my forefinger and thumb together lightly and I slowed down my breathing. Before I knew it, I was at Richmond station and it was time to do this thing! I remained anchored in my intention, and I had a ball.

VISUALISATION MEDITATION
Calm Your Nervous System

The mind-body connection is not felt more vividly than through the power of imagination. Have you heard of the lemon test? It's a visualisation practice where you're instructed to close your eyes, imagine yourself walking to your fridge, taking out a lemon and slicing it into thin juicy slices. Then imagine sucking on a lemon slice. Even though it's all in your imagination, your taste buds start producing more saliva as your body anticipates the sharp, bitter taste of the lemon slice. A guided visualisation meditation is a psychotherapeutic technique that works in the same way as this. What we imagine, the body believes. So if you imagine a deeply relaxing, peaceful scene, your body believes that vision and the relaxation response is activated in the body.

This is a particularly good technique to try if you identify with having a busy mind, as this type of meditation gives the mind a job to do at the start of the meditation. Once the mind has convinced the body it is safe to relax through visualisation, the physiological changes in the body act as a feedback loop to the brain, letting the brain know it is safe to relax further, allowing you to drop into a state of meditation and deep rest. Clever, hey?

A study looking into anxiety reduction found that guided visualisation was an effective method for anxiety reduction, whilst also being a cost-effective method of treatment[7]. Practising this type of meditation can also have a positive impact on depression[8], desired behaviour change[9], and have a calming effect on the nervous system helping you to feel relaxed. It also enhances creativity, problem solving and can even help improve sleep quality.

Benefits: *Promotes deep rest and relaxation; reduces anxiety; improves sleep*

Key features: *Use of imagination and mental imagery*

Length: *10 to 15 minutes*

Frequency: *Weekly*

Tools: *For a guided meditation, you will need to listen to an audio recording*

Best practised: *Listening to a recording*

There are thousands of guided visualisations out there, all offering different takes and themes. The challenge usually is finding a voice that you enjoy listening to. Alternatively, you could record yourself reading the meditation opposite out loud to listen back to.

How to practise this meditation at home

Prepare: Get comfortable, either sitting or lying down. Close your eyes and take three long, slow deep breaths down to your belly.

Step one: Imagine you are standing on a path. It's a beautiful sunny day where the temperature is perfect. Imagine hearing birds singing and the sound of the ocean in the distance.

Step two: Imagine feeling a call to make your way down this path. Notice what you're wearing on your feet, how the path feels beneath them as you slowly make your way down this gently winding path. Imagine that you feel more and more relaxed with every step, feeling carefree, light and calm.

Step three: You notice the path leads down to a magnificent beach, pure white sands and crystal clear water reflecting the spotless sky above. Imagine slowly walking down to the ocean edge, taking off your shoes and walking slowly along the shore line. Watch light sparkle and dance across the water. Listen to the gentle lapping sound of the waves. Feel all cares start to wash away as you feel more and more at ease and relaxed.

Step four: You notice an inviting hammock just up ahead. You make your way to the hammock and wiggle your way in. There's a pillow for your head and shade for your face. You lie back and let your whole body surrender, listening to the sound of the ocean, in this safe, cocoon-like hammock. You shut your eyes and notice the rise and fall of your chest as you breathe easily and slowly. Stay here in this small piece of paradise for as long as you need.

Close: When you are ready to end the meditation, imagine slowly getting up from the hammock, making your way back along the beach, back along the path to the spot you first started at. Take a few deep breaths into your belly, then open your eyes.

Reflection

Having taught meditation for nearly a decade, it became clear to me early on that certain meditation approaches come more naturally to some than they do for others. And this is never more true than with visualisations. I remember teaching an introduction course exploring four different types of meditation in a group setting over the course of four weeks. In week two, we explored focused meditations such as Zen and in week three, we tried out guided visualisations. Both of these two weeks I could almost divide the room in half with those who loved that type of meditation and those who struggled. Some found it hard to focus, bring an image to mind or found themselves over thinking every little detail of the visualisation. While others found it a relief or could vividly visualise and stay with it, without overthinking, easily drifting into deep relaxation. My observations over the years have been that those who are predominantly logical, strategic thinkers find a focus meditation easier, whilst creative thinkers, with a good active imagination tend to prefer visualisations. Neither approach is better than the other, just ways of getting to know ourselves a little better.

DEEP SLEEP MEDITATION
Drift Off

A decent, restful night's sleep is medicine. The benefits of a good night's sleep go much deeper than just waking up feeling refreshed and energised. According to the Office of Disease Prevention and Health Promotion, sufficient sleep not only improves your mood but also lowers your risk of serious health problems. Our bodies release vital hormones during sleep that are responsible for repairing cells and regulating the body's use of energy. When we surrender to sleep, we quite literally hand over control, trusting the magic and wisdom of the body to rest, digest, repair and regenerate, just as we do in meditation. Unfortunately (just as it is with meditation), so many of us find it hard to activate that surrender and to switch off. Insufficient sleep, sleep deprivation and insomnia affect our physical, emotional and mental health, and they are problems on the rise.

Benefits: *Activates the parasympathetic nervous system – rest and digest; promotes deep relaxation; improves sleep quality*

Key features: *Releasing tension in the muscles of the body*

Length: *20 minutes*

Frequency: *Daily*

Tools: *An audio recording for optimal results*

Best practised: *Listened to in bed, ready to drift off to sleep*

There is a sweet spot in our subconscious mind, where sleep and meditation meet. This restorative playground of our subconscious mind can be explained through brain wave states. Brain activity measured by ECG machines shows brain waves ranging from gamma (super fast/high associated with concentration), beta (fast/high associated with wakefulness and anxiety), alpha (slowing associated with restfulness/reflection), theta (slow/low association with drowsiness or deep relaxation) and delta (super slow/super low associated with deep sleep and meditation). When we fall asleep, our brain wave states move from alpha through to theta and delta. It is entering into a delta brain wave state that helps us feel rejuvenated in the morning, and which stimulates the immune system, natural healing and restorative restful sleep. It is there in the 'delta' state where the healing work is done. In meditation, we consciously choose to trust ourselves in the space of suspended thought, dropping into the lower/slow brain wave state. Hanging out there without falling asleep takes practice! The reason it has been claimed that twenty minutes of meditation equates to four hours of sleep is because meditation helps us access those deeper states of consciousness and relaxation. But unlike in sleep, we are still 'conscious' in those states, which somehow seems to turbocharge the benefits.

When we struggle to get to sleep, however, and we need help switching off, meditation can help assist in this transition through the brain wave states, guiding us into a deep and restful sleep. A deep sleep meditation starts with an intention to surrender into sleep.

How to practise this meditation at home

Listening to an audio recording guiding you into a deep state of relaxation is a great place to start. However, it's not always possible to listen to an audio recording, for example, if you're sharing a bed with someone. Having to switch a device off after a meditation has finished can also interrupt the good work that's been done. Instead, be your own meditation guide, and try the following.

Prepare: Set yourself up for a good night's sleep by performing a relaxing sleep ritual before getting into bed every night. Turn all screens off an hour or two before bed and dim the lights. You might like to write down anything that is on your mind in a journal or read a book, whatever helps you start to relax, and draw a line separating day and night. When you are ready to go to sleep, begin by getting as comfortable as possible in your bed.

Step one: Practice mindfulness to notice how comfortable and held you feel – the softness of the pillow, the warmth of the blanket, the feeling of safety, comfort and gloriousness of bed! Really allow yourself to be there, in bed, in the present moment.

Step two: Set the intention to let go of the day you've had, and to drift into a deep, restful sleep.

Step three: Take a long slow inhale, and exhale the breath with a sigh.

Step four: Next, tense all the muscles of the body and hold your breath for the count of three. Really scrunch up your fists, your face muscles, your thighs, the whole body, as tightly as you can before releasing. Repeat this three times, before noticing again how it feels to relax into the comfort of your warm bed.

Step five: Next, take your awareness to the very top of your head and imagine that part of your body melting and surrendering into relaxation. Allow your awareness to melt down through the body slowly, enveloping every part until you reach the tips of your toes, the whole body relaxed.

Close: Feel into the soothing sensation of the chest gently rising and falling, before visualising the number ten in your mind's eye, imagining it slowly disappearing into the distance and darkness. Repeat this with nine, eight, seven... counting down to zero, signifying the moment of surrender to sleep. Let the comfort of the relaxed body and the soothing, rhythmic sensation of the breath be your anchor into deep rest as you allow yourself to drift and fall asleep.

Reflection

The relationship between meditation and sleep is so entwined that they support each other. Regular meditation practice is said to improve the quality of our sleep, and even reduce the amount of sleep we need. There is also evidence to suggest that due to the nature of the cycles of sleep (roughly four hours long), it is not uncommon or even a problem if we find we wake naturally once in the middle of the night. We are often sold the belief that uninterrupted sleep is the best kind but that is not necessarily the case. It is the quality of sleep, or the depth of each cycle of sleep, that really makes a difference. So instead of getting frustrated if you do wake up during the night, can you adopt an 'oh well' approach instead? Frustration prevents you from transitioning back through those brain waves states, and entering into a deep restorative state that is essential for our general health and wellbeing. If you do find yourself waking in the middle of the night, practise the meditation again, instead of getting cross with yourself. Surrender and acceptance are key. Give yourself permission to deeply rest.

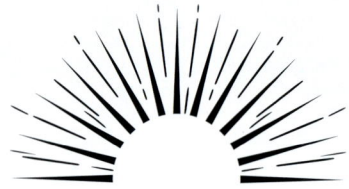

FLOW

Movement Meditations

Inviting the body fully into a meditation practice, moving and shifting stagnant energy held within the body, can allow for a deeper state of meditation to be achieved.

The Meditations

It might surprise some people to learn that meditation doesn't always have to be still and seated. And it's not a requirement for all meditation practices to be serious either! Movement meditations are the practice of being present within the body during a meditative process. They are living, breathing mindfulness practices that allow for a flow of energy to move around and through the body, whilst consciously and intentionally quieting the mind.

Being mindfully in our bodies helps to place us in a flow state – a state where we focus on nothing but the present moment and movement. However, there is a distinction to be made here between sports or activities that get us into a flow state due to a heightened state of adrenaline, when you're 'in the zone', and movement practices that seek to regulate the nervous system and integrate the mind-body-spirit connection. This integration is often referred to as somatic practice.

Thomas Hana first coined the term somatics in the 1970s, explaining that somatics is the study of Self from the perspective of one's lived experience, encompassing the dimensions of the body, psyche and spirit. Yet, somatic practices have been well established since ancient times, with yoga, tai chi and qigong being obvious examples of using the body during practices. The Buddha even taught methods for using the body as a way of coming into a deep state of meditation and presence. Inviting the body fully into a meditation practice, moving and shifting stagnant energy held within the body, can allow for a deeper state of meditation and flow state to be achieved.

There is a phrase that you might have heard – 'you are not your body'. Within some approaches, this phrase is held so seriously that the body is devalued and completely neglected. Whilst there is spiritual truth in the phrase, you are the consciousness or spirit that experiences the body. The body is still how we experience, interpret and navigate the world, physically and spiritually. I often think the phrase should be 'you are not just your body' instead.

DYNAMIC MEDITATION
Integrate Your Shadow

There's a darker side to pop spirituality. One that, although well intended, can and does do more harm than good. Known as spiritual bypassing, it dismisses the reality of difficulties or difficult emotions, and the healing potential of challenging circumstances. Instead of facing these challenges, people might be encouraged to choose 'love and light', but it's really a way into denial.

Meditation is a practice that helps us turn towards ourselves, and uncover the truth of our being in any given moment and situation. There's no running from ourselves in a meditation practice. This is precisely why meditation is intolerable to most people, especially when asked to sit in absolute stillness. It does not provide the body with any means to express the energy of the emotions, trauma and experiences we hold within the body. A dynamic meditation, however, brings the whole being into awareness, including our shadow.

Dynamic meditation is an active meditation practice introduced by somewhat controversial spiritual teacher Osho during the 1970s. A dynamic meditation practice intends to move and shift stagnant energy held within the body in order to break negative patterns or cycles both in the body and the mind. Traditionally, it is a one-hour meditation practised in five stages. One of the first steps is active and intense. It provides a safe and contained space to express emotions, even the most undesirable, like anger and fear. It's a refreshing path of whole-person healing. Instead of trying to rid ourselves of stuck energy or repressed emotions, we are given permission to release them.

Benefits: *Provides emotional release; shifts stagnant energy or trauma trapped in the body; improves emotional and mental stability*

Key features: *Active, intense movement practice before a closed-eye meditation*

Length: *50 minutes*

Frequency: *Daily for two weeks, then take a break*

Tools: *Select a piece of music to dance to at the end of the practice*

Best practised: *With a trained facilitator who can hold space for you, but absolutely fine to practise by yourself at home*

This practice invites what is hiding in the shadows to come into the light, integrating the parts of ourselves that have been dismissed, buried or forgotten. Despite these attempts to lock them away in the depths of our subconscious, they always seem to find a way to manifest in our lives through negative relationship cycles, repeating patterns or behavioural problems. It takes courage to engage in shadow work, and for those who do, liberation is their reward.

How to practise this meditation at home

Osho's dynamic meditation consists of five stages, outlined for you below.

Step one: Breathe deeply and chaotically through the nose for ten minutes. Allow the body to move naturally without conscious decision or control. If the body wants to move with the breathing, let it.

Step two: Allow yourself to make explosive and intense movements and sounds for another ten minutes. Again, allow this to be primal, rather than a conscious thought about what sound to make or what movement to engage in. Let the body move and express itself, and any sounds to come and go without inhibition. Really let go.

Step three: Raise your arms up over your head. For ten minutes, jump up and down, chanting the mantra 'hoo-hoo-hoo'.

Step four: Come to complete stillness. You can remain standing or choose to sit down. Observe thoughts and sensations as they come and go for ten minutes.

Step five: Press play on a chosen piece of music and allow yourself to dance and feel into the freedom of release for ten minutes, before drawing the meditation to a close.

Reflection

It takes courage to face your shadow, and it is arguably an essential part of any spiritual or human journey. In order to allow ourselves to authentically blossom and feel a sense of peace and ease within, we must integrate our shadow, those parts of ourselves or the experience we are ignoring or shutting out. Because that which is hidden always finds a way to sabotage or influence our lives. The shadow is there, whether we face it or not. Shadow work is to take the light of our awareness into the shadow to face what is there. Sometimes we consciously decide to do this. Sometimes life thrusts us in and we experience what is often referred to as 'the dark night of the soul'.

I remember the first dark night of the soul experience I had. It felt terrifying and lonely to wake up in the shadow having no idea how to get out. Asking for help, using tools such as meditation and journaling, making changes and taking small steps each day not only helped me to find my way back to the light but to a deeper sense of connection to myself, others and the world around me. I felt liberated and in love with life. The hardest and best thing to ever happen was to go through that experience. When I face challenges now, I remember it. I can almost enter with a sense of curiosity because I know I will emerge on the other side, and when I do, I will feel even more unshackled and free. If the earth feels like it's crumbling underneath you, please remember you are not alone, and it's okay to ask for help. Hold tight, you will get through this, I promise.

TANTRA MEDITATION
Embrace the Fullness of Life

The Western association with tantra is overshadowed by sex and the *Kama Sutra* but the scope of this healing practice is a lot broader than that. A tantra meditation is concerned with integrating a spiritual journey into all aspects of life, interweaving the physical body, emotions, thoughts and energy into an embodied practice, to live as a full expression of ourselves.

Tantra literally means 'to weave' or 'to expand', and this meditation practice seeks to harmonise the mind, body and spirit to create alignment. Through a tantra meditation, you will explore your divine essence, find a sense of home in the present moment, and recognise the oneness and divine nature of all species of life, including the physical body, so as to expand consciousness. The beautiful thing about this practice is gratitude and appreciation of the physical body it facilitates. With its intricate inner workings of organs and cells, your body is a miracle and a gift. Eyes, ears, touch, taste and smell all allow you to experience life through your senses. Tantra meditation holds the view that the body is a sacred vessel, and should be loved, nourished, nurtured and celebrated accordingly.

Feminine energy is dominant within tantric practices, because the practice seeks alignment and balance between masculine and feminine energies, and for a long time there has been a repression of the feminine. There is a theme within tantric practices to consider life as sacred, including the physical body. It is believed within tantric approaches that suffering comes from the delusion of separation and that celebrating the senses and the simple, daily happenings of our lives is key to liberation.

Benefits: *Promotes grounding, integration and feelings of freedom and liberation; releases stuck energy; awakens consciousness*

Key features: *Integration of body, emotions, thoughts and feelings*

Length: *15 to 20 minutes*

Frequency: *Any*

Tools: *A cushion and a blanket; optional – essential oils or incense*

Best practised: *When you need grounding or a little pick-me-up*

Where other forms of meditation focus on concentration, stillness, abstinence and attempting to get beyond the body, tantric practices invite us to go deeper into the body, and in doing so allow energy to flow and a higher state of consciousness experienced. So, no, tantra isn't just about sex but it does allow for us to include pleasure of all kinds in our spiritual practice and, given the right conditions, sex too can be used as a tool for spiritual growth.

How to practise this meditation at home

One popular tantric meditation is known as Nyasa. Nyasa means to place with tenderness, respect and divinity. For this meditation, inspired by *Nyasa*, you will bring this tender tantric touch to your physical body within your meditation practice.

Prepare: Come into a seated position on a cushion on the floor. Ensure you are comfortable and warm. I enjoy bringing aromatherapy oils into this meditation practice. Find a smell that you enjoy and rub a couple of drops between the palms of your hands and inhale for three long, deep, slow breaths. Alternatively, you might like to burn incense or a scented candle during your meditation.

Step one: Close your eyes and draw your awareness fully into the physical body. Notice how the whole body feels. Consciously soften and relax any tension. Connect with a sense of comfort and safety around and within the body.

Step two: Take your fingertips up to your hairline and hold for a few moments before running the fingertips across your scalp. It might feel nice doing this in a combing motion or with gentle massage movements.

Step three: Next, reach one hand to find the opposite shoulder and hold some pressure on the shoulder for a minute or two, staying connected to your breath. Run the hand down the opposite arm and hold the hand of the arm for a few minutes. Now reach the other hand over to the opposite shoulder and repeat. You might find you sigh a lot – this is a great sign, indicating the parasympathetic nervous system is being activated.

Step four: Next, press and hold both palms over the heart for a few minutes, then the solar plexus (upper abdomen), sacral chakra (lower abdominal space), knees and feet. Allow your own intuition to guide you with all of these movements. Let each touch be tender, honouring the divinity and sacredness of your body.

Close: Sit in stillness for a few moments, with the whole body alive. Feel into a sense of gratitude for the miracle of your body. Close your meditation by placing your hands tenderly over both eyes, before peeling them away to let light in as you open your eyes once more.

Reflection

There is another beautiful tantric touch meditation you could try with someone you trust, a tantric hug! In tantra, the melting hug is used to bring you both into your body as you become fully present with each other. The idea is to hug through your breath, both of you breathing in a synchronised, unifying way. Science is showing that elongated hugs reduce the stress hormone cortisol and increase the feel-good hormone oxytocin. What better combo for a partner meditation practice! If you wish to feel deeply connected with someone, co-regulate and feel good, give a tantric hug a try.

SHAKING MEDITATION
Release Blocked Energy

When the body experiences stress, the autonomic nervous system is activated, the fight-flight-freeze response, which releases adrenaline and cortisol, speeding up the heart rate, blood pressure and breathing. Chronic stress and anxiety, experienced by so many today, is the result of our bodies being in a constant state of fight or flight. When trauma of any kind is experienced, and not processed appropriately, stress becomes chronic and if sustained for long enough our bodies accept the stress state as the norm, trapping our bodies and minds into living in a constant state of stress. It is an overprotective mechanism of the body just trying to keep us safe but is, in fact, causing more harm than good, disconnecting us further from our bodies, always on alert for the next stressor to arrive. Regulation is essential for the body and mind, and shaking can ease an overactive, overstimulated nervous system.

A shaking meditation is the act of letting go. Simply shaking the body activates the parasympathetic nervous system to signal to the brain and the body to relax and let go. On a physiological level, shaking activates the lymphatic system in the body, ridding it of toxins. In a yoga practice, shaking the body out is often used as a warm up exercise, loosening up tension in the body and mind. It appears as a healing practice and ritual across numerous other approaches. One modern approach centred around shaking, called Trauma Release Exercise or TRE for short, was created by Dr David Berceli. It involves triggering 'neurogenic tremors' (shaking) in the body by following a set of exercises, with the intention of re-setting the nervous system and releasing tension and trauma trapped inside the body. One thing for sure is, you feeling great afterwards!

Benefits: *Regulates the nervous system; counteracts the fight-flight-freeze response; activates the lymphatic system*

Key features: *Consciously shaking the body*

Length: *10 minutes or more*

Frequency: *Daily*

Tools: *None*

Best practised: *First thing in the morning or last thing at night, or directly after a stressful/anxious event, situation or mental experience*

How to practise this meditation at home

Prepare: Come to a standing posture, with your feet hip distance apart. Allow your arms to be loose at your sides, your shoulders at ease and your head stacked on top of a straight spine. Very slightly bend the knees.

Step one: Close your eyes. Lean your head very slightly forward. Spend a few moments here to notice how your body feels and perhaps how steady or wobbly you might feel on your feet.

Step two: It doesn't matter where you start in the body but you might like to start with the legs or hands. Just start a shaking movement in the body, allow it to spread and move through your whole body, including the shoulders, head and arms. Engage the breath in the movements too. You might find you naturally want to make a 'haa' noise, sigh or make any other kind of noise as you shake the body out, bouncing up and down on your heels.

Close: Keeping your eyes closed, allow the shaking to start to slow, until you arrive in a still standing posture once more. Spend a few minutes standing still, feeling the flow of energy the shaking has encouraged to move freely around the body. Allow your breath to soften and flow naturally and easily. Notice how you feel – physically, emotionally and mentally.

Reflection

'I can show you what TRE looks like if you like?' my dear friend and TRE practitioner, Jess North, said to me after we'd finished dinner one night at my house. The fire was roaring next to the bright lights of the Christmas tree. She got down onto the floor on her back, and brought her bent knees closer together until they were almost touching, as her legs started to tremble. A gentle shaking movement seemed to move around her body all by itself, from her legs up her back and across her shoulders. 'Are you controlling this?' I asked. 'Nope!' she replied as her arms spontaneously flailed around. Her back arched into a shape and paused for a moment before the tremors continued their journey onwards. It looked bonkers! How could this be happening without her control? I attended one of her classes to try for myself, and she has supported me generously in the practice ever since. From that point on, I've brought shaking of some kind into my daily practice. Whether it is simply shaking out my hands before I sit quietly in meditation, practising a full 20 minutes of a shaking meditation, or lying on the floor to practise TRE. And you know what? I think my nervous system thanks me for it.

CONSCIOUS DANCE MEDITATION
Free Your Spirit

A dancing meditation can go by many names – conscious dance, trance dance, ecstatic dance, to name but a few. A conscious dance meditation aims to access a deep state of relaxation, clear the mind of mental chatter and enter into a deeper, more insightful state of awareness. The aim is to lose your Self to the music, to get beyond the thinking, analytical mind, which can lead to altered states of consciousness. By entering a trance-like state, we are able to bypass the ego mind. Entering this trance-like state seems to be the magic of a dance meditation. It is common to find a trance-like state likened to opening a door of perception or reality. For some, such as Carl Jung, this door leads to what he terms the collective unconscious, a shared, unified field of intelligence outside the reach of the 'conscious' mind. Similarly, in tribal communities, dance is often used in ceremonies and rituals as a means of communication to the spiritual realm.

To enter into the meditation, you dance in an spontaneous way. You simply intentionally choose to allow the body to move mindfully and freely to the sound of music playing. Research suggests that it can reduce psychological distress, process stuck emotions as well as lead to a greater sense of self-expression and wellbeing.

A popular, trademarked conscious dance practice, 5 Rhythms, offers group classes that involve a dynamic movement practice that helps people to be in the body. According to a paper published by The Alef Trust, 5 Rhythms can lead to a heightened state of connection to Self, others and the world. It can help

Benefits: *Clears the mind; increases self expression and relaxation; releases stuck energy and emotions*

Key features: *Spontaneous dance to music or rhythmic sound*

Length: *30 to 40 minutes*

Frequency: *Weekly*

Tools: *Music*

Best practised: *In the evening*

increase self-compassion and creativity[1]. From early morning sober raves to quiet, solo living room sessions and trademarked organisations like 5 Rhythms, the research appears to reveal the same. Move your body freely for long enough, and you will enter a meditative state with psychosomatic healing benefits. You simply have to let go and dance like nobody's watching.

How to practise this meditation at home

Prepare: Find three pieces of music that you enjoy: one piece of music that is of a moderate tempo (ideally 5 to 10 minutes long), another piece that is rhythmic and makes you want to get up and dance when you hear it (ideally 10 to 15 minutes long), and a final piece that is relaxing and soothing (ideally 5 to 10 minutes long). You might like to set up a short playlist for yourself so that one track plays into the next in the order stated above.

Step one: Press play to the first piece of music, and sit or stand for five minutes. Check in with your body. Notice how busy the mind is, what thoughts are dominating the present moment. Notice how it feels in your body – are there any areas of tension? Does your body feel loose and relaxed?

Step two: When the track changes from the first to the next, allow your body to start to move gently. This might be a gentle sway, it might be rolling the head or the wrists. Just notice how the body wants to move. Let the rhythm of the music take hold, letting your body lead the way. Your eyes might be open or closed. You might want to make big expressive movements, or small repetitive movements. It doesn't matter. There is no wrong way to dance. Just let go and feel the rhythm of the music.

Step three: As the final track starts to play, slowly find your way to the ground to a seated or lying down position. Again, notice what the body needs. Allow the eyes to close, as a deep sense of relaxation washes through your body. Drift into a state of meditation, guided by the body.

Close: When the final track finishes playing, stand back up and reorient yourself in your surroundings. Take a moment to honour your body for the practice.

Reflection

In a dimly lit village hall, in a tiny village in Cornwall, about an hour into a conscious dance session, deep in a meditative state, I intuitively found my way down into a squatting position, and I began gently rocking side to side. The music was blaring and I could feel the base was pulsing through my body, almost drawing me deeper into my body, the movement and my meditation. Then, as if from nowhere, tears started to stream down my face. They came with no cognitive baggage, they weren't attached to any story or even a feeling I could identify. With my hands in prayer position, my elbows connected to my knees, still gently rocking side to side in a squatting position, my cheeks become soaked with warm, plump, flowing tears. The release felt kind and from a deep place within me. I wound my way back up to standing and let my body move freely. I felt the hairs on my whole body stand on end. Something had released within me in such a pure way – my body, mind and spirit felt integrated and free.

MINDFUL WALKING MEDITATION
Snap Out of Autopilot

A walking meditation is a fantastic way to integrate meditation into daily life. Most people, who are able to, walk somewhere at least once a day. It might be to catch a train to work, walk the dog or do the school run. Most of our days involve varying degrees of walking. We usually perform this action habitually, with little concentration, especially if it is a route you walk regularly. Without having to really focus, it's very easy to walk these routes from A to B with little awareness, relying on an autopilot state of consciousness to get us there. A walking meditation helps bring a sharp conscious awareness to our experience. It becomes less about the destination or the rush to get somewhere and more about how we engage our senses by using something as simple as our daily walking routes as a tool for meditation.

A formal walking meditation practice is carried out without a destination to get to at all, sometimes round in circles, and is most commonly associated with Buddhist practices. Meditators are instructed to bring their awareness to their feet and very slowly take one step at a time, allowing awareness to move slowly up through the body to the mind. But if the mind wanders during the practice, they might be instructed to pause and start again at the feet. Some techniques suggest synchronising breath with your steps, breathing in as you take perhaps two steps forward, and breathing out as you take three or four steps. Other techniques will encourage you to engage all your senses, to notice the sights and sounds of your surroundings.

One study looked into the effectiveness of mindful walking outside to improve mental health during Covid[2]. Findings showed that improved emotional

Benefits: *Improves concentration, sense of wellbeing and sleep; creates present-moment awareness*

Key features: *Engaging in a mindfulness practice whilst walking*

Length: *Any*

Frequency: *Daily*

Tools: *None*

Best practised: *In silence, even if you're walking with others*

regulation, a sense of wellbeing and the ability to concentrate were all experienced. Interestingly, it also showed an improvement of sleep quality. No matter whether you are able to walk unassisted or you need the use of a stick or a wheelchair, you can still engage in this practice and get an equal amount of benefit from it.

How to practise this meditation at home

Prepare: Identify a route you walk every day. It doesn't have to be a big distance. It could be as short as your walk to the car or as enjoyable as a leisurely dog walk. All that matters is you identify one walk you do every day and set the intention to practise mindful walking meditation for a week.

Step one: Pause before your walk begins. Pause at the front door or pause before you step off the bus, whatever is appropriate to your individual situation. Take a few centring deep breaths. Feel the connection of your feet to the ground. Set the intention to engage your senses and to remain present in the moment – to practise a mindful walk.

Step two: As you set off, bring your awareness to each sense in turn. Notice, for a few moments, the sounds around you – birds tweeting, traffic whooshing by – just notice them.

Step three: Now really connect with what you can see. Really take in the detail of your surroundings. The changing colour of the leaves, the buds and berries, the clouds. Then take your awareness to your nose – notice petrichor, the distinct earth smell after rainfall, for example. Connect to the sensations you feel in your body as you walk. Notice if there is a taste in your mouth left over from lunch or perhaps you're sipping a morning coffee as you walk to work. Then expand your awareness to all your senses and keep them engaged for the duration of your walk.

Step four: Observe when the mind wanders or takes control of your experience. Take a deep breath every time you notice (and if you're a normal human being, the mind will distract you frequently) and switch your senses back on with intention.

Close: Come to a stand still with both feet anchored to the earth, and take a few deep breaths.

Reflection

I pulled up into the car park at the beach in a bright and jolly mood. The dog was eager for his walk. I glanced down at my phone and saw a text message that triggered me, jolting my mood from happy as a sandboy to agitated and infuriated. I slammed the car door shut, chucked my phone in my bag and stormed off towards the beach in a cloud of anger. Halfway along the stretch of sand, I caught myself in the grips of emotion. I paused and looked around. I really saw the crystal-clear blue sea for the first time. Then it was as if my ears turned on too, and I heard the roaring crash of each wave. I looked down at my little dog, who looked back as if to say 'finally, you're here with me'. I had been on the beach for ten minutes but hadn't been on the beach at all. I engaged in a mindful walking practice for the remainder of my walk. Present to all that was there in the here and now, not just my uncomfortable emotions. When I got back in the car I not only felt more balanced but I was able to respond to the text rather than react.

QIGONG MEDITATION
Work with Energy

Qigong, pronounced 'chi gong', was developed as one modality of traditional Chinese medicine (TMC) thousands and thousands of years ago. Qigong translates as 'to work with energy', *qi* meaning 'energy' and *gong* meaning 'to work with' or 'to gather'. It is often seen as a foundational approach from which thousands of other practices have arisen, most notably its close relative tai chi and also martial arts.

The movements involved in qigong are designed to help the movement of energy around the body, optimising flow and energetic balance between the mind, body and spirit. The focus of the qigong practice is to induce a state of meditation and to incorporate breath and visualisations. According to TCM, our vitality is reliant on qi. Energy must flow around the body in order for us to function effectively and feel our best. So often energy becomes stuck in certain parts of the body resulting in pain, illness and disease. A study that looked into 64 people with chronic fatigue found that after four months of practice, the control group who practised qigong regularly during that time reported better mental functioning and less fatigue than a control group of people with chronic fatigue who didn't[3]. Other studies have shown that regularly practising qigong increases certain immune cells, producing a noticeable improvement in immune function[4].

Qigong can be practised internally or externally. An internal practice involves simple movements, breathing exercises and visualisations with the intention of circulating energy around the body, or grounding energy into the earth. An external practice involves passing on energy to others as a form of healing, much like its Tibetan counterpart reiki.

Benefits: *Optimises flow around the body; helps create balance and regulation*

Key features: *Simple, slow body movements paired with the breath*

Length: *Start with 10 minutes and work up*

Frequency: *Daily*

Tools: *None*

Best practised: *Outside*

According to TCM, qi flows through the 12 meridians of the body, which are energy pathways that are associated with each organ, with half of those meridians being yin (feminine energy) and half being yang (masculine energy). An internal practice of qigong seeks to ensure there is an adequate flow of qi through all 12 meridians.

How to practise this meditation at home

Prepare: Start by standing tall, feet hip width apart, knees ever-so-slightly bent so they're not locked. Close your eyes and notice the stability of your body in this simple standing position.

Step one: Then begin a gentle bouncing motion on your heels. Bouncing up and down, with your arms and shoulders relaxed. Spend a few moments doing this, eyes open or closed, it's up to you. Then start to gently swing your arms from side to side. Ensure your feet are rooted into the earth.

Step two: When you're ready, come back to an easy standing posture. Take a big deep breath and raise your arms up and out wide, ensuring your arms are at the top above your head at the top of the in breath. Imagine you are gathering qi or energy as you scoop your arms up. Then on your out breath, allow your arms to come down the centre line with your palms facing down and your fingertips pointing towards each other. Imagine that you are grounding qi and energy as you draw your hands down to the earth. Repeat 10 times.

Step three: Next, hold your right hand palm facing up, almost as if you're holding an imaginary ball. Then as you breathe in, sweep the arm across the front of your body up above and beyond the left shoulder. As you breathe out, allow the palm of the hand to face down as you sweep it back down to the original position. Repeat on the opposite side with the left hand. Repeat 10 times.

Step four: Finally, stand in a slightly wider stance. With both hands, imagine scooping healing water up in front of you, bringing it up the centre line, palms facing up as you breathe in. Then imagine throwing the water up into the air as you turn your palms down and lower the arms down and out wide as you breathe out. Repeat 10 times.

Close: Bring your body to stillness with eyes open or closed. Notice a sense of steadiness in the body, breath and mind.

Reflection

Midway through a ten-day silent vipassana retreat (as described in the Awaken chapter) we were gifted 20 minutes of qigong during one break time. I say 'gifted' because it truly, deeply felt like a gift to my body. Every day for the duration of the retreat we sat on the floor in silent, still meditation. Alongside the abstinence of speaking, eye contact, reading, writing, distractions of any kind, we were also instructed to abstain from any physical movement other than gentle walking, no running, no dancing, no yoga. My body ached. Qi was certainly not flowing freely. The body is seen in so many traditions as something to get beyond and not to integrate into a spiritual experience. We practised a few simple qigong movements, paired with breath. The tiny hairs covering my body stood on end, something that happens when qi moves around the body, as I later found out. I felt a rush of bliss.

TAI CHI MEDITATION
Balance Yin and Yang

Much like qigong, tai chi involves a series of slow movements, breath work and posture to move energy around the body and induce a meditative state of mind. What differentiates tai chi from qigong is actually a little tricky to decipher. The most obvious way to tell them apart is that qigong involves repetitive and simple movements, whereas tai chi tends to offer sequences that involve the whole body.

There are five main practice styles of tai chi with distinct variations: *yang*, which involves slow movements and balance; *wu*, which includes a lot of forward and backward movements; *chen*, the closest form to martial arts; *sun*, which focuses on footwork and can look a bit like dance; and *wu (hao)*, involving a more internal focus. All styles aim to bring the practitioner to a state of wholeness and fosters an inner peace.

A growing body of research suggests that tai chi is an effective treatment for the prevention and rehabilitation for a number of conditions that are associated with ageing[5]. It's also a beneficial treatment for autoimmune diseases that involve pain such as fibromyalgia.

Some of the movement meditations featured in this section allow the intuitive body to guide the movements, whereas tai chi is a practice of engaging the mind, directing the body and harmonising a mind-body-spirit connection. Movements are relaxed, synchronised and performed in a state of hypnotic flow. It is a deeply calming and grounded form of movement meditation, where all parts of the body and mind are engaged in a mindful manner.

Benefits: *Improves balance; reduces stress; helps to balance yin and yang*

Key features: *Low impact, slow, synchronised movements performed mindfully*

Length: *20 minutes*

Frequency: *Daily*

Tools: *None*

Best practised: *In a group*

How to practise this meditation at home

Prepare: Come to a standing position with your weight distributed equally on both feet. Allow your arms to be loose and relaxed by the sides of your body. Close your eyes and feel your energy ground down into the earth.

Step one: Keeping your wrists and hands relaxed, raise your arms up out in front of you to shoulder height as you breathe in. Your fingertips will naturally be pointing downward with your hands and wrists fully relaxed. As you breathe out, lower your arms back down to a relaxed position by your sides. Repeat this gentle easy movement, aligned with each inhale and exhale for twenty rounds.

Step two: Now shift your standing posture so that your left foot is slightly in front of your right, both feet facing forward. As you breathe in, reach your arms forward in front of you and transfer your weight over to your front foot, allowing the heel of the back foot to slightly lift. Allow the palms of the hands to face each other and although your arms are extended forward, allow them to remain soft, with a slight bend at the elbow. On the exhale, transfer your weight onto the back foot, with the toe of your front foot slightly raised, as you open out your arms wide, broadening your chest. Ensure your shoulders remain relaxed as you do this. Repeat this gentle rocking motion, synchronised with your body and breath, twenty times.

Step three: Next, come back to a relaxed standing posture with your feet hip width apart, and your weight balanced equally on both feet. Bring your hands in front of your body and close your fingertips together as if holding a big round ball. On your next inhale, draw the palms of your hands up until they reach chest height. Turn the palms of the hands over, so they are facing down, and on your exhale lower then back down. Repeat this twenty times.

Close: In tai chi, the end of one movement is the beginning of the next. Be conscious of this transition as your close your practice – it is the beginning of the next activity. Can you bring the same sense of mindfulness and presence to that, as you did in this movement meditation?

Reflection

Sat in a stark room in a fertility clinic, dressed in a light blue hairnet and a hospital gown that ties up at the back, exposing your bare bottom to anyone walking behind you, I was waiting to be called in for another attempt at an IVF frozen embryo transfer. My brilliant acupuncturist suggested tai chi while I waited. So I rose to my feet to practise five minutes of tai chi. I anchored down into my feet, being kept warm by fluffy socks and I remembered the earth beneath me. I raised my arms up above my head and gathered energy down as if pulling it down into my body. I scooped my arms out wide as if drawing energy into my body, before sending it back down to the earth. The sensations of anxiety and racing thoughts I had experienced five minutes before eased. My breath was steady, my body, mind and spirit felt like they were coming into alignment. All parts of me felt grounded, relaxed and ready.

YIN YOGA MEDITATION
Rest and Restore

What a lot of people don't realise is yoga is a form of movement meditation, traditionally practised as a way of preparing the body for a seated closed-eye meditation. In today's world, where people are so often seated at desks, in cars or on the sofa watching TV, it is not surprising that energy in the body gets stagnant. Moving from any of these seated postures into a still, seated meditation practice might not always be the most beneficial. Any yoga practice, no matter the approach or school of thought, is a means to unite the mind-body-spirit, and the physical postures are a means of shifting stuck energy to allow a seated meditation. Yoga even translates as 'yoke' or 'union'. The discipline of yoga spans philosophy, breathwork, mantra, meditation, a huge range of postures, mind, body and spirit connection and practices, and enlightenment. There are hundreds of different approaches and styles. Yoga also involves rich texts and philosophies that encourage a yogic way of life.

The style of yoga most commonly associated with meditative states is the practice of yin yoga, as opposed to the more 'yang' or energetic styles of yoga that are dynamic, constantly in motion and physically challenging. Yin yoga is a slower, more restorative set of postures. It is a passive sequence of postures that are held for three to ten minutes at a time. The idea is that you meet your physical edge in a posture, and soften into it. It allows you to ease into the connective tissues of your body rather than to work the muscles in more yang approaches. It is working with the deeper connective tissues that is said to be the source of release for trapped emotions in the body too. Ample research has shown the positive effects of a simple yin yoga practice on the mind and body.

Benefits: *Boosts circulation; improves flexibility; reduces stress and anxiety; helps release emotions locked in the body*

Key features: *Holding restorative yoga postures for extended periods of time*

Length: *20 minutes*

Frequency: *Daily*

Tools: *Yoga mat, two pillows/cushions or a bolster, a blanket and a timer*

Best practised: *In a class with a trained instructor*

In order to safely and comfortably soften into the edges of your body, it is helpful to practise with some supportive tools. A yoga mat, a blanket and cushions or pillows are sufficient. If you have a bolster, even better. Although it can feel a little uncomfortable meeting your edge, you should never be in pain or discomfort. The use of comfortable props helps to avoid this.

How to practise this meditation at home

Prepare: Have a timer to hand, and gather any comforting tools you have access to, such as a blanket, pillows and a bolster.

Step one: Come down to your yoga mat into child's pose – sit back onto your heels and open your knees out wide, walk your hands out in front of you, drawing your chest closer to the ground between your knees. Allow the palms of your hands to be flat on the mat. Close your eyes and connect to your breath. It might feel nice to cover yourself with a blanket in this pose. Stay here for five minutes.

Step two: Next, come up to a seated position on your mat and bring the soles of your feet together into a butterfly pose. Allow your knees to open wide and adjust the positioning of your heels to ensure you can find your edge without discomfort. This posture might be enough, or you can fold at the waist drawing your chest down towards the mat if you want to explore deeper into the pose. It might feel good to place pillows or cushions under the knees in this pose. Close your eyes and stay connected to the breath. Stay here for five minutes.

Step three: Now come back up to a seated position with your legs stretched out straight in front of you. You might find it more comfortable to sit on some cushions or a block so your sit bones are raised up a little higher. Soften the knees slightly (you also might like to put a blanket under the knees) and when you're ready, fold at the waist drawing your chest down towards your thighs. Close your eyes, stay connected to the breath. Stay here for five minutes.

Close: Lie back down on the yoga mat on your back ready for the final pose, savasana. Here, you might like to cover yourself with a blanket, put a bolster under your knees or a pillow under your head. Allow your legs to be hip width apart and your feet flopped out to the side. Allow your arms to be slightly away from the body. Close your eyes and stay connected to your breath. Stay in this position for five minutes.

Reflection

I remember being introduced to yin yoga for the first time when I was in Costa Rica. I had been chatting to the studio owner whilst in the café below the yoga studio. I was in Costa Rica to look after horses and I was riding most days. My body was toned and fit but my flexibility was poor. 'You should come to our yin class' the Costa Rican yoga teacher said. 'It sounds easy but it's actually really hard'. She explained that it was holding the same posture for five minutes and that it can often bring up all sorts of emotions. I agreed to give it a go. Fifteen years have passed and yin remains my favourite yoga discipline. The slow, restorative, deeply feminine nature of the practice is what my mind, body and spirit often yearn for. It allows for a deep connection to my body, and a deeper state of meditation at the end.

BECOME

True Self Meditations

Your true self isn't some future version of you, a new and improved version of you. It isn't a polished, shiny, perfect version of you. Your true self is the self who is sitting here now reading these words.

The Meditations

Meditation, much like hypnosis, can help us access and work with our subconscious mind. Through regular, consistent meditation practice, we cultivate the skill of self-knowledge and self-trust. We become more of who we truly are.

Your true self isn't some future version of you, a new and improved version of you. It isn't a polished, shiny, perfect version of you. Your true self is the self who is sitting here now reading these words. The self that allows yourself to feel what you are feeling, to say what you are thinking, to want whatever it is that you want. And to love the life you are living.

This collection of meditations holds an intention to help you reconnect to your true essence. You will journey through a series of meditations that will help you overcome fears, integrate your inner child and your elder self, and explore what it might mean for you to drop the mask and let your true self shine. A lot of these meditations involve visualising and working with the subconscious mind as a way to facilitate new connections and pathways between mind, body and spirit.

Authenticity means you are being genuine with yourself and others. You are being your truth. In doing so, you might find it is a lot easier to set loving boundaries, to break unwanted patterns or cycles and to make conscious decisions aligned with your deepest values, desires and truth. Pretending to be someone else, people pleasing and self-abandoning are often strategies employed out of fear of being rejected or abandoned. You might keep quiet, not speak up and claim something that you deeply desire for fear of being ridiculed or cast aside. The further we journey away from ourselves, the more confusing and disorientating it can feel. You are your own best guru, teacher and guide – I hope these meditations will help you realise that.

Becoming your true self is a practice of self-knowledge and self-trust. You might like to see these meditations as sign-posts and tools to help guide you back home to yourself. Give yourself permission to be who you are. You are welcome. You are worthy. You are meant to be here now, so shine bright.

LOVING KINDNESS MEDITATION
Feel Connected

Loving kindness meditation, sometimes known as metta meditation, is a centuries old Buddhist meditation practice that helps facilitate compassion and benevolence towards yourself and others. A lack of compassion leads to disconnection, whether that's disconnection from ourselves, from others or the world. It creates a sense of dualism and 'other', which leads to fearful reactions, judgements or choices and blame. All of which are some of the ego's favourite traits! Lacking compassion and kindness is a path to loneliness, isolation and bitterness, there's no doubt about that. What we can't see or accept in others is often what we can't extend to ourselves (extreme moral examples aside, of course). When we are able to empathise and show compassion we dissolve an invisible barrier between 'Self' and 'other'.

Benefits: *Boosts mood; soothes self-criticism; increases social connection*

Key features: *Use of affirmations and intentions to increase feelings of compassion and kindness to self and others*

Length: *15 minutes*

Frequency: *Daily*

Tools: *None*

Best practised: *First thing in the morning and/or last thing at night*

Loving kindness meditation is a well researched approach to meditation. Numerous studies have shown that even a simple practice can reduce depressive symptoms, increase feelings of self-acceptance, reduce stress and ease self-criticism, even in the most self-critical amongst us[1]. There is also a strong link between a loving kindness meditation and increased social connectivity[2].

A fascinating study was carried out over three months, which looked at the impact of a loving kindness meditation on those suffering from PTSD. The results showed a reduction of PTSD and depressive symptoms, and increased feelings of self-compassion[3]. I often wonder, if people truly loved and accepted themselves, would they cause intentional harm to others? One study found that self-compassion was one of the key features in lowering criminal impulsiveness and increasing self-control among imprisoned inmates[4].

Extending kindness and compassion to others helps us to feel good about ourselves. And the better we feel about ourselves, the more kindness and compassion we seem to be able to give, and the better choices we are able to make. It seems to be a mood-boosting, self-fulfilling prophecy that leads to a greater sense of connection.

How to practise this meditation at home

Prepare: Settle into a position, either sitting or lying down, with your eyes closed. Take a few centring breaths. Relax the muscles of the body. Drop your awareness down into the heart space, and breathe in and out from the heart space for a few moments.

Step one: With a connection to your heart, bring to mind someone you have deep, unconditional love for. It might be a child, a partner, a family member or a pet. Hold them in the mind's eye of the heart. Feel and connect to the deep sense of love and gratitude you have for that person. Imagine sending them love and kindness and repeat the following affirmations in silence in the mind and heart:

- May you be well
- May you be safe
- May you be happy
- May you find peace with whatever is happening
- May you accept yourself as you are

Step two: Next, bring to mind a friend who you have fond feelings towards. Hold them in your mind and heart, sending them loving kindness and repeat the affirmations above.

Step three: Now bring to mind a 'neutral' person. Someone you don't know that well or even by name. It might be a local café worker or someone you'd recognise from work but don't know. Send them loving kindness and repeat the affirmations above.

Step four: Next, bring to mind someone you have challenging feelings towards. To the best of your ability, repeat the affirmation above and send them your loving kindness.

Step five: Now bring the whole planet into your awareness. Imagine your awareness expanding to include the oceans, expanding across the land and all creatures, and the sky. Hold all beings in your heart and send them loving kindness, by repeating the affirmations above.

Step six: Finally, bring yourself to mind. Extend the same kindness, love and compassion towards yourself. Let it fill up through your bones, your cells and your mind. Repeat the following affirmations:

- May I be well
- May I be safe
- May I be happy
- May I find peace with whatever is happening
- May I accept myself as I am

Close: When you are ready, take a deep breath and open your eyes.

Reflection

In the early days of teaching meditation, I ran a weekly class at the local university, mostly attended by the hard working staff and some PhD students. Each week we would practise a different type of meditation during their lunch break. One week, a PhD student looked tired and a little withdrawn. I checked in with her before we began. She was in the middle of a breakup, where her life had turned upside down and the steady ground beneath her feet felt as if it had crumbled away. I invited her to go gently through the loving kindness meditation practice, as we settled down to begin. Afterwards, she shared that it wasn't the part of the meditation where she extended kindness towards her ex that she found the hardest. That, she said, felt somehow freeing, leaving her feeling a little lighter. It was the part where she had to extend loving kindness to herself. She realised all the blame and shame she had been carrying. It was compassion for herself that she most needed.

INNER CHILD MEDITATION
Heal Old Wounds

Inner child work is a vital component of spiritual growth and a personal journey towards wholeness. The term 'inner child', coined by Carl Jung, offers a metaphorical representation of a time during childhood when developmental programming happened within us that shaped our current reality as an adult. No matter how wonderful a childhood might have been, there will always be that one experience, that one bully, that one teacher, that one moment, that made you feel embarrassed, ashamed or frightened, resulting in you then believing something negative about yourself or the world. We then unconsciously carry that belief through to adulthood. Perhaps it's a belief that you're not good enough, not smart enough, not welcome, or it's a belief that you're too loud or too much. As children, we just want to feel seen, loved, validated, accepted and safe. All sorts of experiences can lead to us not feeling this way. Inner child work gives us a tool to trace back to those crucial times in our lives, and reprogramme our present-moment reality.

There are many therapeutic approaches that involve some form of inner child work – internal family systems, rapid transformation therapy and matrix re-imprinting, to name but a few. An inner child meditation can be a great option to begin or deepen inner child practices. If you are aware of acute traumatic experiences, it might be helpful to find a trained meditation teacher who can hold space for you and guide you through a meditation. Whether you're practising alone at home or with a professional, it's true to say that inner child meditation can be powerful, and even when practised multiple times, a different experience will often be had. A different memory, a different belief or sometimes the same one but on a deeper level may be processed. It's important to remember that the past no longer exists, all that is real is the present moment, right here, right now. Meditation can help us access the present moment, and inner child work can help us reprogramme our mind and body to not believe it is still in the past. The practice of inner child work can also be called re-parenting, suggesting we are re-parenting ourselves with the love, reassurance, acceptance and safety we may have been lacking through childhood.

Benefits: *Promotes psycho-spiritual healing; strengthens sense of self-connection, empowerment and autonomy; being able to set clear and loving boundaries*

Key features: *Visualising oneself as a child during meditation*

Length: *10 to 15 minutes*

Frequency: *Once a month*

Tools: *None*

Best practised: *With a guide or someone to hold space for you as you practise and after you've practised*

How to practise this meditation at home

Prepare: Start the meditation in a comfortable seated position, with your feet flat on the floor. Take a deep breath and on the exhale, close your eyes. Take your awareness down to the feet, and feel into the connection of your feet to the earth. Let this connection symbolise a sense of grounding and safety, rooting you firmly in the present moment.

Step one: Relax the whole body. Feel your shoulders drop away from your ears. Unclench the jaw and soften all the muscles in your face. Allow your belly to be soft. Rest your awareness on your natural breathing for a few moments. Notice the soothing rhythm of each breath arriving and releasing.

Step two: Allow yourself, in your mind's eye, to arrive at a time and place from your childhood. Notice how old you are, where you are, what situation you are in. See if you can vividly hold the memory and your younger self in your awareness.

Step three: Imagine stepping into the memory and walking up to your child self. Imagine looking into their eyes, and notice if it feels right to reach out and hold their hands or to embrace them. Notice how your inner child wants to interact with you. Get a sense of what it is your inner child needs to hear at that moment. Imagine looking them in the eye and telling them what they need to hear. Notice what else they might need. Maybe it's to sit with them, play with them, or embrace them again. When you're ready to leave, imagine looking your inner child in the eye and saying you love them.

Close: To bring yourself back into the present moment, take a deep breath and draw your awareness into the physical body. Feel the feet connected to the earth and the breath move through your body. Place your hands over your heart, and seal in the love and acceptance you just practised with yourself. Open your eyes and take your gaze around the space you are in, taking a moment to anchor fully back into the present moment. You may wish to journal your thoughts into a notebook, share the experience with a friend or loved one, or keep it as a special experience between you and your inner child.

Reflection

'I'm here' I softly called to my inner child in a guided inner child meditation one day. She was sitting on her childhood bed, arms cradling her knees, refusing to acknowledge I was there. I knew she could hear me. I knew she knew I was there. 'I'm going to come and sit next to you, okay?', I said in my meditation vision, as I moved slowly closer to her and sat next to her. I sat with this image. Just me as my adult self, sat there with my inner child, both of us not saying anything at all. After ten minutes, I could feel her starting to thaw. I imagined putting my hand on her knee and felt her lean in closer to me until she melted into my arms. Tears flooded down her cheeks in the visualisation and down mine as I sat there in meditation imaging the scene. Something inside me thawed and integrated. The meditation helped me to unlock and repair some part of me that felt shut out. It still remains one of the most powerful visualisation meditations I've ever experienced, and it will be something, I'm sure, I'll carry with me forever.

ELDER SELF MEDITATION
Feel Guided

What if, in the same way there is an inner child part of ourselves, there is already an older, wiser self with grandmotherly or grandfatherly qualities? The part of us who knows and accepts who we are, is wise to the challenges and the magic of the journey of life unfolding. Not a future self we might envisage or wish to manifest, but an elder, a sage or a crone, who has lived and learned.

Hindsight is a magnificent gift, isn't it? We're able to look back and see the path we've taken so clearly. We are able to identify when we made decisions in alignment with our authentic truth and when we didn't. We are able to see each twist and turn, every crossroads, even blind-siding events, and how one choice led to another, that led to another, that led you to the person and place you are today. Hindsight is a portal to acceptance and wisdom on the deepest level. Hindsight reminds us we are not in control of all that happens to us yet we do have agency over how we respond. It is our choices, thoughts, beliefs, and how we respond to life as it shifts and evolves, that changes the direction of our lives, as if we were blindly adjusting the sails in the moment. Through hindsight we gain wisdom, as we look back and learn from all that's been before.

We often come across the question 'What advice would you give your younger self?'. When we flip the question to ask 'what advice would your elder self give you?', time and space seem to collapse, and we are able to tap into the energy of hindsight in the present moment. We are able to tap into our own innate wisdom.

Researchers have found that projected future self states have a motivating quality[5]. In meditation, we are able to narrow the gap you might feel between the

Benefits: *Promotes self-soothing; connects with inner wisdom; ignites inner guidance and direction; builds self-trust*

Key features: *Visualising yourself as an elder*

Length: *15 minutes*

Frequency: *Once a month*

Tools: *Blanket; optional – background music, notepad and pen*

Best practised: *In the evening when you can completely relax*

wisdom of your elder self, and with who you identify with now. Some researchers use the term 'future self-guides'[6], which is exactly what you can expect to experience practising this meditation; a feeling of being guided by the wise elder part of yourself that already exists within. You can practise this meditation at any age, to connect with deep wisdom, calm and surety found within.

How to practise this meditation at home

Prepare: Get yourself into the most comfortable position you can. Dim the lights, grab a blanket and you might like to play some soothing instrumental meditation music in the background.

Step one: Take a few deep breaths and scan your body for any tightness, gripping or tension. Relax the whole body and allow your awareness to rest on your breath for a few moments. Watch and feel into each soothing, calming, rhythmical round of breath.

Step two: Bring to mind the space you are in and imagine seeing yourself exactly as you are, right here in this moment. Then imagine your elder self walking into the room and slowly moving closer to you. Allow your own imagination to guide the journey. You might imagine your elder self sitting next to you, or you might embrace. Whatever comes and feels right to you is the right thing. Notice how it feels to be in their loving, accepting presence. Feel into the sense of wisdom and compassion they exude. Spend a few moments here, feeling their willingness to be with you and to exude love and kindness to you, as you are right now.

Step three: Imagine looking them in the eye and asking for some guidance or asking them a question of any kind. Allow a response to come. Ask whatever you like and however many questions as you feel called to.

Step four: Imagine them placing their beautiful wrinkly hand over your heart space, and receive the love and connection into your heart. Notice if they want to say anything else before they leave. Watch them walk back out of the space and bring yourself, as you are, back to mind.

Close: Connect back to your breath, then back to your body. Take a deep breath as you gently blink your eyes. You may wish to journal or reflect upon anything that came up.

Reflection

Sprawled out like a starfish in my garden one hot summer's afternoon, I practised an elder self meditation, guided by an audio recording made by a beautiful teacher and author called Lynette Allen. I was a couple of weeks into a three-week online women's circle hosted by Lynette. The women's circle held the powerful intention of gathering and integrating three archetypal parts of ourselves: the girl we once were, the woman we are today and the woman we're yet to become. I settled back on a blanket, put my earphones in and pressed play on the recording. My elder self entered into my meditation and came and lay next to me on the earth. She placed a beautiful wrinkly hand over my heart, looked at me with sparkly, life-filled eyes and said 'My love, I'm not going to tell you anything. Just keep trusting yourself and you'll see how it all plays out. Oh, you will see!', she said with a playful smile. I thought I wanted to hear concrete advice, specific guidance on how to get and achieve what I wanted but as it turned out 'keep trusting yourself and you will see' was exactly what I needed to hear.

UNBLOCK CREATIVITY MEDITATION
Create with Ease

By the very nature of your existence, you are creative. Every thought and every action you take is a creative process. The *Oxford English Dictionary* defines creativity as 'the use of imagination or original ideas to create something; inventiveness'. We tend to experience creative blocks when we are being overcritical of ourselves or when we over-think something. Our logical 'thinking' mind seems to get in the way of allowing this imaginative, creative energy to flow through. Meditation is the perfect tool for engaging a different part of our brain to logic and 'thinking'. I like to think of it as clearing the weeds of the mind to create space and tranquillity. From the space created, we can allow a natural flow of creativity, trust and love to bubble up or burst through.

A creative block is really just the over involvement of the thinking critical mind. This part of our mind is very useful and required in this human life but it doesn't have to be in the driving seat all of the time. Putting pressure on ourselves to be creative is one sure way to prevent it. Surrender, achieved through meditation, allows for it to come through naturally. Numerous studies have shown that there is a link between meditation and an increased sense or output of creativity. Meditation opens up the mind to new ideas through something called 'divergent thinking'. This is particularly true when exploring studies that are concerned with the connection between mindfulness meditation and creativity[7].

It's helpful to consider the different ways in which our brains work. Some areas of the brain are responsible for analysing logic, are concerned with facts and are the parts of the brain that think in words. Other areas are responsible for imagination, feelings, sensing, interpreting and a more integrated, holistic way of thinking. Creativity is achieved when there is a balance

Benefits: *Relaxes the mind; boosts creativity, focus and problem solving*

Key features: *Visualising clearing to allow creative flow to enter*

Length: *10 minutes*

Frequency: *Any*

Tools: *Optional – notepad and pen*

Best practised: *When you experience a creative block of any kind*

between all of these parts of the brain, especially when in a theta brain wave state, precisely the things meditation helps facilitate. One of my favourite stories involves Russian chemist and teacher, Dmitri Mendeleev. Feeling frustrated with trying to come up with a way of organising elements into a scientific sequence, he decided to take a short nap. Short naps, like meditation, allow brain wave states to drop into that magical meditative theta frequency. During his nap, he had a vision where he saw all the elements falling to place. He scribbled the sequence onto the back of an envelope as soon as he woke up. And so the periodic table was born.

How to practise this meditation at home

Arguably all types of meditation help to unblock creativity but here is a meditation that can be practised at those times when you're experiencing a creative block. Alternatively, you could take a nap!

Prepare: If possible, practise this meditation outside. If not, and it's safe to do so, you might like to open a window and let some fresh air in.

Step one: Come to a comfortable seated position, this might be on a bench or directly on the earth. Ensure your back is upright, your shoulders are relaxed and soften your arms and hands in whatever way feels comfortable.

Step two: Take a few moments to allow the breath to anchor you into the present moment. Follow the effortless rhythm of the breath. Notice the sensations that move through the body from your nostrils, throat and chest. Notice how the lower belly gently expands and contracts with each breath.

Step three: Allow your awareness to rest outside of the body for a moment. Feel into the space directly around the body, the space your energy takes up. Imagine that space expanding and contracting with each breath too, just as your physical body does. Imagine that energy held around the body starting to soften and dissipate. Feel into the vast space around you – space that has no limits. Become aware of the vastness of the cosmos above your head. Notice any breeze or sensation of air touching the skin as movement of energy, keeping a freshness to this moment.

Step four: Breathe into the whole body, including the mind, and imagine that vastness and freshness of energy and space to be mirrored within. The vastness of consciousness, life and love. Allow each breath to attune to the space around and the space within. Stay here for as long as you need.

Close: To close your meditation, become aware once more of the earth beneath you. Place your hands on the earth if you're able to, or focus on your feet connected to the earth. Feel a sense of steadiness, security and rootedness being here in this body, supported by the earth. Start to open your eyes and mindfully gaze around the space that you're in. Notice the tiny details, the colours and textures as you allow a smile to come to your face.

Reflection

What is consciousness? Since it's not something that can be put under a microscope and dissected, science can only present a hypothesis, just as mystics and philosophers do. Is consciousness generated by the brain, as a function of biology? Or is the brain the receiver of it, like a radio? The same question could be asked about creative sparks and ideas. Are they really ours, generated from within our biology? Or are they channelled, received from elsewhere? According to the literary legend Elizabeth Gilbert, ideas float around and wait for someone to receive them. In her brilliant book *Big Magic* she warns that you must take action on this creative spark when you receive it otherwise the idea moves on and finds someone else. Have you ever had an idea that you didn't take action on, perhaps due to fear or negative beliefs such as 'who am I to do this?', only to find that, months later, someone else is bringing that exact same idea to life. Creativity, ideas and imagination are gifts of the human experience. Something to cherish, nurture and give space for. Who are we to get in the way of that, hey?!

AUTHENTIC SELF MEDITATION
Live Authentically

There is a brilliant Lao Tzu quote that goes 'Watch your thoughts, they become your words; watch your words, they become your actions; watch your actions, they become your habits; watch your habits, they become your character; watch your character, it becomes your destiny'. When our thoughts, words and actions are in alignment we are embodying our authentic selves. It is the version of you that is free from self-imposed restrictions shaped by fear or insecurity, free from fear of what others might think, free from the pressures and expectations society, family or friends might put on you to conform or be a certain way. Being your authentic self is to be who you truly are without any masks or shields.

For a lot of people, especially people pleasers, self-abandoning themselves and their authenticity is an adaptive strategy performed in order to fit in or to be validated. Perhaps this need to be included and accepted is coded somewhere deep in our DNA. In hunter-gatherer communities, not being accepted or exiled would have meant being cast out in the world alone, and would have certainly led to a fateful end.

The further away from your authentic, true self you venture, the more you question your own thoughts, feelings or choices. You aren't able to trust yourself because you don't know who you are. The real you is hiding behind a mask. Interestingly, the origin of the word 'authentic' derives from an old Latin word meaning genuine. It requires vulnerability to drop the mask, to be who you truly are as you move through this life. It is truly liberating to be around people who are wholly genuine and who embody their authentic selves.

Benefits: *Promotes a balanced and healthy view of self; increases self-awareness and self-confidence; helps develop a sense of self-empowerment; facilitates calm and ease*

Key features: *Visualising your true self*

Length: *10 minutes*

Frequency: *Every few months*

Tools: *Optional – notepad and pen*

Best practised: *Being guided by a teacher*

Numerous studies show that being authentic is linked to increased positive states of psychological and emotional wellbeing. One study looked at the effects of being authentic on teen mental health, finding a strong positive correlation between a feeling of being 'happy to be me' and reports of a healthy sense of wellbeing[8].

In visualisations, like the one opposite, you might be surprised at the wisdom and clear guidance your true self offers you. What you must remember is that wisdom or guidance came from within you – that wisdom *is* you! Your truth and intuition is always there ready to guide you, but might just need to give yourself permission for the real you to shine through.

How to practise this meditation at home

Prepare: Get into a comfortable position and do whatever you need to do to allow yourself to drop into meditation. This might be stretching, shaking your hands out, or spending a few moments focusing on your breathing.

Step one: When you are ready, close your eyes and imagine you're standing at the end of a long corridor. Imagine the corridor is a place that you feel very safe and comfortable in. You feel gently drawn to start walking slowly down the corridor. Notice what it looks like: what type of corridor it is, are there any windows, doors, plants, paintings?

Step two: As you slowly walk down the corridor, imagine a door up ahead that you feel really drawn to. Imagine walking up to the door and very slowly opening it. Behind this door is the most beautiful space. Let your own imagination conjure up the space – is it indoors or outdoors? What is in the space? What does it smell like or are there any sounds? Allow yourself to explore this beautiful, perfect, peaceful space in your own time.

Step three: Imagine seeing someone standing in the middle of the space, and as you turn towards them you realise it is you. It is your authentic self. Imagine slowly walking up towards them. Notice how they are standing, the smile on their face. Notice the peace and softness in their eyes. Notice what they are wearing, how they are holding themselves and get a sense of how it feels to be in their presence.

Step four: Imagine looking down and noticing they are offering you a gift. Accept the gift without analysing it. It doesn't need to make sense, just notice what is being offered. Next, ask yourself for a piece of advice on something that is challenging you, you're trying to make a decision on or just want some guidance on, and notice what reply is offered.

Step five: Take one last look at your radiant, beautiful, whole self and then imagine stepping into their shoes, looking out from their eyes, standing right where they were standing because they have been you all along. Notice how it feels to be standing there, integrated with that vision of your authentic self.

Close: Take a deep breath and imagine walking as your true self back through the space you were in, slowly back out the door, and back along the corridor to the place where you first started. With that connection to your own truth, wisdom and radiance, take another deep breath and open your eyes. You might wish to journal your reflections after this meditation. What might the gift symbolise? What advice did you receive? How did it feel seeing yourself as your true self? How can you embody them in daily life?

Reflection

I remember feeling so detached from my authentic self I had no idea who I truly was anymore. I couldn't even remember what I genuinely enjoyed, what made me tick or come alive. I felt so exhausted by holding a mask up to the world, using all the remaining energy I had to try and fit in. It took a breaking point and coming to meditation for the very first time to start the journey back home to myself. A journey that might last a lifetime but one that I am eternally grateful for. To give ourselves permission to be who we truly are is liberating. It's honouring the gift and sacredness of being given the opportunity to be here now and experience it all.

PROTECTION MEDITATION
Safeguard Your Energy

Boundaries are a hot topic in the self-development world, and for good reason. Setting healthy boundaries is an essential skill for embodying good self-care but it can be a real challenge for the people pleasers amongst us. A healthy boundary creates a clear limit to how we wish to be treated. This might include physical, emotional or psychological boundaries, or it might include our time and energy. I remember reading something once that said 'boundaries show people how to love us'. I love that. Boundaries aren't creating walls around ourselves, isolating us from deep connection but instead they are deeply personal limits ensuring we are not self-abandoning, exhausting ourselves or people pleasing.

A protection meditation helps us shift our mind set to be better able to uphold these deeply personal boundaries and to share them with others. It also helps us go deeper and protect our energy. Have you ever had an experience where you feel completely exhausted after hanging out with a certain person, as if they have drained you of all the energy within your heart, mind and body, leaving you feeling empty. Meanwhile, they might remark – 'Gosh, I'm feeling so much better now, full of life'. There is a term used to describe these people – energy vampires! They knowingly or unknowingly drain you of your emotional energy by taking advantage of your willingness to empathetically listen or be there for them. Sometimes even a hug from an energy vampire can leave you feeling completely depleted. We all go through hard times and sometimes take more than we can give but with an energy vampire it is only ever take, take, take.

Benefits: *Protects energy; upholds healthy boundaries; connects to your truth*

Key features: *Visualising a protective shield around the body*

Length: *10 minutes*

Frequency: *Whenever required*

Tools: *Smudging sage or other native herbs; optional – music*

Best practised: *In a quiet space alone before going into a challenging situation*

A protection meditation is a technique often used by healers or holistic therapists before a session to help energetically shield themselves. It is also a technique used by psychologists. There are always going to be people or situations in our lives that challenge us. Using a protection meditation before you go into a big scary meeting or meet up with that challenging someone who you suspect is an energy vampire, can help us remain centred, protected and able to lovingly uphold our boundaries.

How to practise this meditation at home

Prepare: Consider listening to some soothing instrumental music or mantra music that instantly transports you to a relaxed state to begin your meditation. I like to look for a 1111 hertz track to play whilst practising this meditation but find something that works for you (see the Sound Healing Meditation in the Regulate chapter for more on this). Burn sage or other native herbs to cleanse yourself and the space you are in.

Step one: Sit in an upright position with space around the whole body. Breathe into the heart space, the solar plexus (upper abdomen), the sacral chakra (lower abdomen) and the root chakra (hips and pelvis). Feel the steadiness of the body where you are sitting.

Step two: Feel into the energy around the body, just around and outside of the skin.

Step three: Imagine a forcefield of energy surrounding the whole body, acting as a protective layer around you. You can imagine this forcefield as a colour, perhaps white or a soft pink, whatever works for you. This protective shield acts as a filter that allows love, kindness, support and authentic connection to flow freely in but protects you from negative energy, words or intent. Such things simply bounce off the protective layer and are not permitted to enter in. Anything that you need or choose to be released is able to leave freely but your energy can not be taken from you without your permission.

Step four: Allow every breath in to strengthen this beautiful protective shield, and let every breath out be loving. Sit in this visualisation for as long as you feel the need to.

Close: When it is time to close your meditation, open your eyes and still imagine or feel into a protective layer around you. Know you can take this protection with you throughout your day. If you need to re-engage with it, take a deep breath and bring this protective shield to mind.

Reflection

I paused in the loos before returning to join someone at a lunch table. I'd visited the loos to take a break in the conversation rather than needing the facilities. I stood in the cubicle and steadied my breath. I played a song you can find on Spotify called *Trigger Protection Mantra* by Jhene Aiko on my headphones. I closed my eyes and practised this protection meditation for just two minutes, re-centring myself, and reminding myself of my boundaries before heading back out to face the music.

ANCESTRAL HEALING MEDITATION
Break the Cycle

Rooted in indigenous traditions around the world, including paganism and shamanism, the importance and prevalence of ancestral connection is starting to gain traction in modern psychology, integrating itself into therapeutic approaches[9].

We all know that we carry the same DNA as our ancestors. It is clear to see physical characteristics and attributes being passed down from generation to generation. What you might not be so aware of is that patterns and trauma are also passed down through generations, known as transgenerational trauma. All this is passed down on a subconscious, cellular level, which is why you don't need to have known your ancestors in order to benefit from this meditation, although knowing their story can sometimes help the puzzle pieces slot into place more easily.

Whether this is a brand new concept, or you are deep in your healing journey, it requires self-awareness, knowing your own patterns and traits, fears and aversions. Some make sense in our own lifetime – we were let down as a child and now expect to be let down as an adult, for example. But if there's something that appears a little more puzzling to you, something you can't quite place to explain why you are the way you are, perhaps it has something to do with ancestral trauma. It could be an ancestral theme of feeling like you don't belong, for example.

This meditation is concerned with ancestral healing, which is something that goes both ways. It's a practice of carrying on lineages of positive traditions, feelings and characteristics and it is a process of cycle-breaking negative or damaging ones.

Benefits: *Helps emotional healing; promotes self-empowerment*

Key features: *Visualising receiving support and cutting energetic cords*

Length: *30 minutes*

Frequency: *Infrequently*

Tools: *Candle, sage or a smudge stick, a flower of your choice, a photo or symbol of an ancestor whose attributes you cherish and admire; optional – music*

Best practised: *In a circle of trusted friends*

To be a cycle breaker is to consciously choose to face, explore, forgive and heal ancestral patterns. It is not about judging or condemning but instead about forgiving and freeing that which is holding you, and holding those before you, back from living a full, rich and vibrant life. Through the process, you not only break the cycle of generational patterns that are resulting in unwanted experiences, you also gather lost parts of yourself back. What a gift to yourself and to future generations!

How to practise this meditation at home

Prepare: Gather a candle, sage, a smudge stick or incense, a flower of your choice and a photo, symbol or trinket that represents an ancestor or role model. When you're ready to begin, light the candle and cleanse the space you are in by burning the herbs or incense.

Step one: Breathe into the heart space and connect with the safe, kind, loving energy found within. Spend ten minutes or so reflecting on patterns, cycles or any repetitive negative relationships that are present in your life that you wish to break the cycle of. Identify key people, stories, situations or feelings within you associated with these.

Step two: Reflect on ancestral guardians who have had a positive influence on your life. You don't need to have met them to deeply feel this. Identify the qualities and attributes you associate with them.

Step three: Place your photo or symbol and flower in front of you, side by side as an offering to them. Close your eyes and breathe deeper into the heart space. Steady your breath and turn inward for meditation. Bring to mind and call forward the ancestor or guardian who has had a positive influence on your life. Feel their love, support and protection surround you. Imagine a cord extend from your body that is attached to the cycle you wish to break. It might be connected to a specific person, event or feeling.

Step four: With the support of your guardian, imagine seeing that person, event or feeling through compassionate, loving eyes. Whisper internally, directed towards the cycle you are breaking 'I set you free. I set myself free. I am choosing another way. I am free'. And imagine unplugging the cord from your body and it disappearing into the abyss. Imagine your guardian placing their love, protection and guidance over the space of your body where the cord was attached, healing it with light and love. Say thank you and smile.

Close: To close your meditation, you might wish to listen to a piece of music that feels empowering, nourishing and kind. Sit in stillness with music playing for the duration of the song before taking a deep breath, opening your eyes and blowing the candle out.

Reflection

Sheltering from the lashing rain in a rustic barn on the banks of the River Fal in Cornwall, I huddled in a circle with 13 other women. I had the privilege of holding space for them on a weekend retreat exploring and reconnecting to our wild nature. Each brought with them a symbol of their ancestors or guardians who had had a powerful influence on their lives. We placed these sacred items in the middle of the circle, scattering rose petals and carefully placed lit candles amongst them. After we had taken turns, witnessing each other share vulnerability of the cycles we were breaking and the ancestry support and strength we wished to carry through, we sat closer together and held hands. As if through divine intervention, with perfect timing, a beautiful song called *Rose* by Ayla Schefer started playing…

'We are woman, we are bringers of life
We are vessels of love, we are expressions of
the divine
Sister hold my hand
In this circle we remember
Sister hold my hand
You are stronger than you know'.

Tears streamed down our faces. The cycle breaking had begun.

BEYOND FEAR MEDITATION
Move Forward

Fear takes many forms. Some fears are rational, based in the physical world where the consequences, if it all goes wrong, are quite obvious – fear of heights or deep water, for example. Fear, in this instance, is a mechanism of trying to protect us from physical threats. This kind of 'rational' fear also presents itself in very obvious ways. For example, we freeze and are unable to physically take another step forward.

Other types of fear seem to be a lot more subliminal and discreet. These are the types of fears that aren't based in an objective reality. They are subjective and often so buried in the subconscious that they are hard to even put a name to. A fear of closeness, or fear of success, for example. These types of fear manifest in subtle and confusing ways. Perhaps our conscious mind only becomes aware of them through the repetitions of unwanted cycles or situations. Fear of any kind can hold us back from living a full, meaningful and happy life whilst at the very same time, fear can also be one of the greatest teachers.

Through reflection, or through psychotherapeutic support, most of our emotional or psychological fears can be traced back to an earlier experience in life, often in childhood, which is where inner child work can be extremely poignant, or through ancestral healing. But some fears are accumulated along the journey of life, right up into later life. Fully understanding the root cause of those fears is often the key to overcoming them. But nearly all fears are caused by our thoughts. The self-knowledge cultivated through meditation is a powerful place to start when seeking to overcome fear.

Benefits: *Creates self-knowledge; builds self-awareness, self-trust and self-respect*

Key features: *Being the witness to your thoughts, especially fearful ones, and the use of affirmations*

Length: *10 minutes*

Frequency: *Daily*

Tools: *Optional – notepad and pen*

Best practised: *Last thing in the evening*

Through regular meditation practice, we are able to be with our thoughts as a loving witness. And we practise getting comfortable with the uncomfortable. It is through mindful presence that we are more likely to be attuned to our own bodies' reactions and responses to our own thinking, including fear-based thoughts. Through this ability to be with what's there, we somehow are able to transform through it. When we have the courage to face or move through our fears, they often dissipate in the process, and we realise they were an illusion all along. What would you let yourself do if fear wasn't holding you back?

How to practise this meditation at home

Prepare: Come into a seated position with your feet flat on the floor. Soften your shoulders away from your ears. Relax your arms and have your hands placed comfortably in your lap. Allow your breath to be relaxed, rhythmic and even.

Step one: Take your awareness down to your feet. Feel a connection to the earth and feel supported, stable and secure, right here in this moment.

Step two: Practice for a few moments just being with your thoughts. See if you can be a witness to them, watching them flow in and out of your awareness like fast and slow moving vehicles. Notice when one of those thoughts has swept you up as if you're travelling in the vehicle. Relax back into awareness, taking a deep inhale any time you need to reset.

Step three: Practise the art of getting to the contents of your mind without judging yourself or making any part of you wrong. Just sit quietly with your thoughts. Some thoughts will be based on fear, some will be based in judgements, while other thoughts will be kind and encouraging.

Step four: Next, bring your body into your awareness. Notice any physical sensations or reactions occurring within the body. Establish a relaxed, soft body as a foundation. Notice when tension or sensation arises.

Step five: Repeat the following affirmations silently in your mind or out loud. 'I am safe.' 'I am learning.' 'I trust myself.' 'I am not my thoughts but they are something I experience.' 'I choose now to no longer be afraid.' 'I no longer believe the fearful thoughts that are holding me back.' 'I am free.'

Close: Place both hands over the heart in a loving gesture. Take a deep breath into the heart space as you draw the meditation to a close. Set the intention to weave this practice and the affirmations through each day, to notice thoughts and witness them rather than get swept along by them, to notice bodily reactions and sensations and to consciously soften and relax. Set the intention to remind yourself of these affirmations often.

Reflection

Lying in bed next to a guy I was seeing, I felt paralysed. We'd had an awkward intimate moment that didn't end well. He reacted by rolling over and turning his back to me. Lying on my back, hands tight in fists against my chest, eyes wide open, I could not sleep. I wanted to be anywhere but there but I felt frozen in my own bed. It felt as if the house was burning down yet I couldn't move. I was triggered into the freeze response.

Later the next day, after we said goodbye amicably, I sat in meditation curious as to what was going on internally for me in that experience. I identified a chain of fearful thoughts: Men don't want me in their life. I am not good enough. It is not safe to be myself. I identified fourteen fearful thoughts that were looping around my mind the previous night, thoughts that activated the freeze response in my physical body. I decided to write out the opposite of those thoughts and to see how those flipped beliefs might feel. I read through the list of fourteen now positive affirmations and it was as if all the cells in my body began to vibrate in a new way. What if I believed these thoughts instead, I thought to myself. How differently my patterns, choices, reactions and behaviours would be. I recorded myself saying them and listened to it every night before I drifted off to sleep, helping to reprogramme my beliefs and transmute fear.

SELF-FORGIVENESS MEDITATION
Release Your Prisoners

Self-forgiveness is a challenging and complicated pursuit. To accept flaws and weaknesses, and be able to forgive ourselves for our mistakes, requires a profound level of wisdom to realise it is a gift to others and the world, as well as to ourselves, when we do. We've all done things in the past that we're not proud of and given a second chance, we wouldn't do again. What if I told you, despite that thing, and despite the way you judge and condemn yourself for it, you are enough. You are worthy of love and forgiveness.

Self-forgiveness doesn't mean not taking responsibility for your own actions. It is not saying what you said or did was right. It's not a passive process. It is an embodied choice to allow all parts of you to be present and integrated into your experience of who you are today, including the parts of you that are scared, angry, fearful, ashamed or damaged. Self-acceptance is gathering scattered pieces of yourself back and accepting your weaknesses as well as your strengths. It is about integrating your ego, your inner voice of fear or your inner critic, not rejecting it. It requires letting go of shame and guilt and instead developing a sense of self-compassion.

One study looking at self-forgiveness explored a four-step therapeutic model. The research suggested that taking responsibility, having remorse, focusing on restoration or making amends and starting afresh was a successful approach to achieving self-forgiveness[10].

Self-forgiveness is about letting go of fear, blame and shame. You might consciously not forgive yourselves as a form of self-punishment, perpetuating shame and guilt. Those murky emotions reside right in the dark depths of your subconscious mind. Self-forgiveness is an act of taking true responsibility. It requires you to name what you did wrong and to say sorry for

Benefits: *Releasing shame and guilt; building a sense of self-compassion, self-trust and self-awareness*

Key features: *Visualising releasing those you have not forgiven and releasing yourself*

Length: *15 minutes*

Frequency: *When needed*

Tools: *Some soothing meditation music and a blanket*

Best practised: *In the evening when you can dim the lights*

it. Without self-forgiveness, can we really make amends? We are all learning, evolving human beings who sometimes get it right and sometimes make mistakes. We are all the same in that respect, all of us. Self-forgiveness is actually a gift to those we love and to the world too. It means we can love more deeply and unconditionally, and move through the world with more ease and purpose. Forgiving yourself is a journey and a process, and as with all journeys, it starts with an intention to begin, and one first step.

How to practise this meditation at home

This is an adaptation of a meditation taught by author and spiritual teacher Janet Conner. The intention here is to forgive others and yourself.

Prepare: Lie on the floor, bed or sofa. Place a comforting blanket over you. Dim the lights and you might like to play some soothing, restful meditation music in the background. Close your eyes and relax your whole body.

Step one: Imagine you are standing in front of a large, old, heavy door. You push the door open and notice a dirty, dark staircase winding downward. You move slowly down the stairs and notice a pungent smell. The walls are dripping. It's cold and dark. You make your way to the bottom of the staircase.

Step two: You notice a row of old, dark prison cells that are barely lit. You walk up to the first prison cell and take a look in. You notice, sitting on the floor, a person you've been holding prisoner in your own mind. You lock eyes with each other and you don't say a word. You open the cell door and motion for them to stand up and walk out. Set your prisoner free. You get to the next prison cell and notice someone else. You again motion them to their feet, open the door and without a word set them free. Repeat this as many times as you feel called.

Step three: When you have emptied all your prison cells, you turn as if ready to leave but notice one more cell. Smaller, darker and more hidden than the rest. As you walk up to this cell, you look in and realise the prisoner is you. You beckon them to the stand as you open the cell door wide. You beckon them again and say 'It's okay. It's time now. I set you free.' Imagine watching as they leave, being cleansed by the light as they transcend up the staircase.

Step four: Imagine the whole dungeon transforming and flooding with light. Every cell, including your own, is now bathed in healing, purifying, radiant white light. Imagine making your way back up light-filled steps as you make your way back to where you first started.

Close: Take a moment to anchor back in the body. Place your hands on your heart and feel the cleansed sense of light and love within your heart. Open your eyes and take a while to look around and anchor yourself back into this reality.

Reflection

Holding yourself prisoner might feel like just punishment, judged by the jury in your mind. Is it that by not forgiving yourself, perhaps everyone will know how sorry you truly are? Is it a fear that by forgiving yourself, you are excusing or justifying your mistakes? Forgiving yourself isn't a sign of weakness, it's a measure of a strong character. It doesn't mean you're letting yourself off the hook, it means you're taking responsibility. It is a springboard from which you can redirect your life to make better choices and to choose love. It's time now, and it's okay to let go.

ALIGN

Mindful Living Meditations

*These meditations are
a way of taking what
we learn on the cushion
into our daily lives.*

The Meditations

You might find that the meditations in this chapter are a little different to the rest. The idea of these meditations is to weave the principles and qualities of many formal, seated, closed-eye meditation approaches into everyday life. To use them when your eyes are open, when you're fully engaged and participating in the external world, navigating all its wonders and challenges. Nestled within this chapter, you're going to explore simple, enjoyable practices that will help you align your life with your core values, so to live and breathe meditation throughout your daily life, making life itself a meditation.

It is true to say that these meditations require work, discipline and commitment but luckily it is of the gentlest, most playful kind. Mostly, they require a ginormous dollop of self-compassion. There are times when you will remember and it will feel as if you are living in full alignment; when you are able to embody these practices and feel great for doing so. And there will be other times when you forget; when you will get caught up in the tangled web of fear and judgement, or be drawn into the unconscious trance of the mind. And do you know what? It is absolutely fine when you do – it is to be expected. You are human after all! Just as you will practice with seated, closed-eye meditations, the practice isn't about perfection. The art of meditation is noticing when the mind has wandered and in that noticing to consciously return your awareness to whatever anchor you are working with, the breath for example. This same principle is applied to these mindful living meditations. You will practice being the loving witness of the inevitable cycle of remembering, forgetting and remembering again. These meditations are a way of taking what we learn on the cushion into our daily lives in order to live with a sense of alignment with life itself.

So many of these practices are about letting go of resistance, yielding to and saying yes to life as it is. They are also about humility and trust. These simple practices will help you get out of your mind and into life, enabling you to experience a greater sense of ease and flow, as if you are moving with life, rather than against it. These meditations should, in essence, feel like relief. A way of truly knowing you are right where and who you're meant to be, on this wild, miraculous journey of life.

BEGINNER'S MIND MEDITATION
Experience Awe

The Zen Buddhist practice of 'beginner's mind' is a meditative practice of weaving childlike curiosity into everyday life. It is also known as *shoshin*, a Japanese phrase meaning 'to remain open', present and aware through all our experiences.

In a closed-eye version of this meditation, a beginner's mind might look like simply arriving at your meditation with curiosity, as if sitting in meditation for the first time. It's not about bringing preconceptions or judgements with you but instead a gentle, open awareness that allows you to be willing to see what is there within your experience, in each unfolding moment. This is an especially powerful practice for seasoned meditators.

A beginner's mind in daily life fosters a sense of childlike curiosity, intrigue and wonder, even when faced with the most mundane activities. It is to practise experiencing each day as if for the first time. Not in a false, forced, contrived way, of course, but with the loving intention of letting each new day and experience surprise you. Imagine turning up to a date, regardless of how long you've been dating, with this attitude. Dropping baggage filled with assumptions and judgements before you begin. When we are beginners at something we are open to learning, willing to be surprised and assume we don't know all the answers, all of the time. A closed mind becomes clouded with assumptions and leads to a lack of motivation, interest or excitement in life. Greeting each new day with a closed mind can be a spiral into feeling like you're in a rut. Choosing to greet each day, and meditation, with a beginner's mind, we are more likely to be present, open, grateful and aware.

Benefits: *Renews interest in life and all things; increases sense of awe, gratitude, openness and awareness*

Key features: *Bringing a childlike sense of curiosity to all experiences*

Length: *Woven throughout the day*

Frequency: *Daily*

Tools: *None*

Best practised: *Starting the day by setting an intention*

An interesting and rather niche study looked into the practice of beginner's mind in middle school mathematics students. It found that the students who brought a beginner's mind to mathematical problems were more able to think about them more deeply and problem solve more creatively[1]. Another study, which zoomed in on two specific qualities of a beginner's mind, mental reframing and awe, found positive correlations with a reduction of depressive symptoms as a result[2].

I like to see the practice of beginner's mind as the gateway to embodied mindfulness or mindful living. It forms an anchoring intention from which the practice of mindfulness is then possible.

How to practise this meditation at home

Let go of preconceptions

Whether you decide to practise this type of meditation as a closed-eye practice or woven into your daily life, or both, a good place to start is to identify what your preconceptions are before you begin. Then imagine letting them go, clearing them from your view, like cleaning the lens of your glasses, before you begin your day or your meditation.

Slow down and engage your senses

A core principle of any mindfulness practice is to slow down, to attune to the pace of the natural world and to engage your senses. Let sounds, sights, tastes, smells and touch be an anchor into the vast, open space of the present moment.

Adopt a sense of childlike curiosity

When we move slower and are more present in our surroundings, we naturally notice more. The magic and miracle of the natural world comes alive and into view. You might notice the poetry of dew drops on a spider's web on your morning commute, or the dance of light across a body of water on your dog walk at dusk. Children are masters at noticing the intricacies and wonder of the world around them, present to the colours and textures of life. Become curious, without judgement or over-thinking. This same sense of curiosity and playfulness can be brought to self-reflection, noticing emotions, thoughts and feelings in and out of a closed-eye meditation practice. The same state of witnessing can be brought into our daily lives as we begin to notice with curiosity our behaviours, actions, habits and words.

Let yourself be surprised

Showing up to your day or meditation practice with openness shifts you into the role of learner rather than expert. It opens you up to new possibilities and carries with it the energy of a soft, playful whisper to the universe to surprise you.

Reflection

Have you ever noticed that most of us are masters of mindfulness, with an eager beginner's mind, when we are on holiday? We seem to notice the different aromas and sounds. We really taste the flavours of the different foods as we explore with our senses wide open. We savour each day, squeeze the juice out of the experience and as a result feel fantastic for it! What if you applied this same sense of curiosity to everyday life? What if you let the ordinary, wonder-filled life you get to lead surprise and delight you?

I remember returning home from a life changing trip to South America that completely altered the way I viewed the world, and how I felt within myself. It was as if the veil had been lifted and I could see the magic, wonder and mystery of the world once more. I was determined to not slip back into old ways once home. I identified various different things that would help me remain mindful and live each day with a beginner's mind, something I could so easily do overseas. I decided to get rid of my TV and set the intention to read more; to embed a meditation practice into my daily routine; to explore where I live as a tourist would; to take a different route home when I could. And I decided to dial up self-compassion any time I'd forget or slip back into old habits. I've found that this has to be a conscious daily practice. Something that gets renewed every single day, and in every moment. It doesn't seem like a chore but a wonderful gift of starting again afresh when I remember.

EMBODIED MEDITATION
Live in the Present

Embodied mindfulness is a state of being. In simple terms, it is the process of becoming more of who you truly are, while finding a sense of home and safety in the present moment. To embody anything, requires you to live in alignment with it. To breathe, move, walk, talk and behave as it. An embodied mindfulness meditation practice leads to a deeper knowing and acceptance of yourself and the world around you. The practice will help you to understand the language of your body and the complexities of your mind, almost as a way of transcending the foggy view of yourself and life that the thinking mind alone would have you believe. Instead, life becomes a full-bodied, holistic and sensory experience, enabling you to live more deeply and authentically. Embodiment means living your truth in any given movement.

A meditation practice of any kind is not asking you to be anyone or anything other than who you are. It is the foundation of the deepest acceptance. The practice of embodied mindfulness asks you to witness and allow any sensations in the body, emotions or feelings to be there. To be present with them as they bubble up and pass through our experience. In doing so, you are better able to detach your identity from the feeling or sensation and stay in the seat of awareness. The more practised you are at that, the more able you are to live each day in this way, in flow, in a state of calm, firmly anchored into the present moment. It is a shift from the over-involvement of the mind to a practice that activates the senses and incorporates the whole body.

Benefits: *Promotes a whole-person approach; develops self-acceptance*

Key features: *Living and breathing mindfulness in all experiences in life*

Length: *Continuous flow of practice*

Frequency: *Daily*

Tools: *None*

Best practised: *As a way of life*

'Being' is a term often given to this embodied state, where we're ultra present in the moment, when you are really here, in the now, in the reality of your experiences ('good' or 'bad'). 'Being' doesn't mean standing still doing nothing, relaxing or being passive. It is to be ultra present as you move through all the responsibilities, challenges, experiences and daily doings of your life. It is to have a regulated nervous system and a present state of mind that manifests as clarity, focus, inner calm, satisfaction and a high state of creativity.

How to practise this meditation at home

Witness your reactions

Become the loving witness to how you react to events, people, circumstances or change as you move through your day. Watch as you react, or reflect afterwards. Were you reacting out of fear? Was it a defensive reaction? What part of your self-identity were you defending? How did it feel? Where did you feel it in your body?

Witness your habits

As above, start to witness the habits you might have previously unconsciously been a slave to. Notice your choices and decisions as if sitting in a seat of all-seeing, loving awareness. Be curious as to why you are doing or choosing what you are. Is it really something you want? What purpose is it serving in your life? How does it feel to engage in it? Embodied mindfulness helps us identify habits and start to make small steps in the direction of change, reinforcing habits that serve our highest good and moving away from those which don't.

Be in the body

Watch how the body responds to life. When a stranger is rude to you for no reason, notice how your body reacts. When your partner doesn't do what you want them to, notice what happens in your body. When life surprises you with something wonderful, notice how the body responds. Embodied mindfulness is the practice of noticing without judgement as a means to integrate and align the wisdom of the body into your everyday life.

Reflection

There is a popular phrase that gets used a lot on social media which encourages us to 'be rather than do'. Although well intended, this simple phrase can often lead to the misconception that mindfulness or 'being' is passive. Or it suggests that we have to decide between the two states – we can either 'do' or 'be'. But being and doing are not polarities. Doing is an essential part of life. It always has been and always will be. When we don't see these two states of being as opposites, we find a sweet spot that becomes available to us. Magic and peace are found when we master the art of both – being as we do. 'Being' is an ultra state of presence as we move through our lives. The 'doing' becomes much less stressful and much more enjoyable when we are present and open. When I remember this – the power of being as I do – it makes life feel safe and fluid. I naturally move slower, notice more, make more conscious decisions and choices, hear what's truly being said, and set clear and loving boundaries. Being as I do opens me up to more enjoyment, and life seems a little less serious and a little more playful.

ACCEPTANCE MEDITATION
Be with What Is

The scope and influence of acceptance runs so deep and wide, it can affect almost all aspects of life. There is the tricky business of self-acceptance or accepting others the way they are. And there is the challenge of accepting things as they are, especially when they are not to our liking. Acceptance isn't giving up, settling for or being a doormat. It isn't passive. As mindfulness master Jon Kabat Zin says, 'acceptance is an active process', it requires your conscious participation.

Acceptance also doesn't mean we don't work towards change, quite the opposite. It means we deeply recognise where we are, accepting the situation we are in, so that we know how and where to take a conscious first or next step. Before you can work with or process anything, you must first acknowledge and accept that it's there. In many ways, acceptance gives rise to conscious action and to much more measured and wise responses. Life, people or things might not always be to your liking, but it is true to say, in any given moment, it is the way it is.

Buddhist meditation teacher and author Tara Brach talks of radical acceptance in her book of the same name. She claims that acceptance is the gateway to all that we are so often seeking – love, wisdom and peace. To fully understand this, it can be helpful to consider what the opposite of acceptance is – denial or resistance. When we are in a state of non-acceptance, refusing to accept something the way it is, we are at odds with it. This creates friction and tension and we expend an enormous amount of energy, exhausting ourselves in the process. We are at odds with reality and not in alignment or flow. When we live in a state of resistance, we are perpetuating the unwanted reality we are not facing. Tara Brach encourages us to ask ourselves when we recognise we're in this state of resistance 'Can I be with this with kindness?'.

Benefits: *Reduces stress; improves emotional regulation; improves coping mechanisms*

Key features: *Identifying and releasing resistance*

Length: *10 minutes*

Frequency: *Any*

Tools: *None*

Best practised: *When in a state of resistance*

Acceptance is to be present in reality as it is, to allow what is there to be there. From that clarity you can consciously choose to surrender, to be with what is with kindness, or to take action and initiate change.

How to practise this meditation at home

Prepare: Settle into a meditation posture of your choosing. Close your eyes and breathe deeply to anchor yourself in the present moment. Soften the body and feel the sensation of the breath moving through the body. Rest your awareness for a few moments on the heart space as a way to come into a state of intimate communion with yourself.

Step one: Whilst being gentle with yourself, reflect for a moment on an aspect of yourself or your life that you are in resistance with. This might be a quality, a desire, a habit, ageing or some part of your physicality, or a situation, person or experience. Reflect on what it is you are resisting and how the resistance is playing out in your life. Identify any stories your mind might be telling you to reinforce this resistance. Recall how it feels to be in a state of resistance, and where you feel that feeling in your body. Imagine that resistance as energy and notice what colour that energy is.

Step two: Take a long deep inhale and imagine breathing out the colour, releasing the energy of resistance from your being. Repeat a few times – this is a gentle and loving way of clearing yourself out.

Step three: Reflect now on how it feels to be free of resistance and free from any narrative attached to it. Notice what remains. Flood your body, mind and heart with an energy of acceptance, love, compassion and kindness and affirm silently in your mind or out loud 'I love and accept myself as I am'.

Step four: Place your hands on your body intuitively in a way that feels kind and anchoring – it might be holding your hands on your heart or belly, cupping your face with your hands or placing your hands over your eyes. Allow feelings of relief, flow and acceptance to rise and be present.

Close: Take a long, slow, deep breath before closing your meditation.

Reflection

From a young age, I have struggled with a healthy sense of self-worth and self-acceptance. As a teenager, I would rehearse negative and damaging affirmations to myself over and over. This mostly criticised my body and the way I looked. Years later, I started to practise what author and spiritual teacher Louise Hay called 'mirror work'. Looking at myself in the mirror every day and affirming my love and acceptance. It felt beyond uncomfortable to start with, and wholly untrue. But I stuck with it – affirming my acceptance of myself, my face and my body, as I am. It started to get a little easier and I started to notice subtle changes in the way I felt about myself.

One night, brought to my knees in resistance with a reality I did not want to face, I caught a glimpse of myself in the bathroom mirror. My eyes were puffy and my face blotchy red from crying. In an instant, the old well rehearsed narrative launched itself – affirming how ugly and unworthy I was. Witnessing those thoughts, I paused, took a breath and anchored back into reality. I looked at myself in the mirror again and affirmed out loud, 'It's okay to feel this way. I love you, and accept you as you are. Especially now. As I am. As things are. I chose to accept and be here with kindness'.

The grip those emotions had over me started to soften. My shoulders relaxed away from my ears. My breath became steady – I re-found the safety of the present moment. I felt an inner sense of connection and peace, and an outer sense of clarity. From the safety of the present moment, we can move forward with a greater sense of ease, no matter the circumstance.

GRATITUDE MEDITATION
Feel Good

'Gratitude changes everything', so they say. But does it, really? According to an ever-growing catalogue of research, and personal accounts from regular practitioners, it appears that it certainly can change a lot. Scientific studies are proving that neural functional connectivity in the brain changes when gratitude is intentionally practised, wiring our brains for greater emotional regulation, self-motivation and reducing states of anxiety and depression[3]. And there is an unquantifiable amount of accounts in wellbeing and spiritual podcasts and blog sites claiming an improved sense of general wellbeing with a regular gratitude meditation. There is undeniably something magical in it.

In truth though, that phrase is somewhat paradoxical. A gratitude meditation or a gratitude practice doesn't necessarily change anything externally at all. Our problems don't miraculously vanish, and situations or people don't change to our liking because we practise gratitude. Instead, it is the lens through which we see the world that changes. It is this internal shift that holds incredible, life-changing, life-affirming power.

Practising gratitude helps us find a sense of emotional balance in a world that is challenging and complicated. It doesn't take away our problems but it helps us remember the good things that exist, and no matter how dark and how bleak it gets, there are always some. Shift our focus towards the light, and in doing so the light grows. It just feels good.

Psychologists see gratitude practice as a way to strengthen positive recall bias, which counterbalances the natural negative bias we humans have been wired to adopt through evolution. In a world that wants us to keep wanting more, it leaves little room for gratitude for what we already have. There will be so much in

Benefits: *Improves emotional regulation and self-confidence; reduces stress and anxiety; creates feel-good vibes*

Key features: *Bringing to mind and feeling the emotions associated with the things we are grateful for*

Length: *10 minutes*

Frequency: *Daily*

Tools: *Optional – notepad and pen*

Best practised: *First thing in the morning or last thing at night*

your life that you have now that you once wished, hoped and dreamed for. A gratitude meditation is about viscerally recalling the good that surrounds you, really feeling that love, support, sense of achievement or comfort found right here in the present moment.

How to practise this meditation at home

Prepare: Get into a comfortable seated position with a straight spine. Take a moment to look around the space you are in with mindful presence. Really allow yourself to anchor into the right here, right now.

Step one: Take a few deep belly breaths and allow the eyes to close. Take the palms of your hands to your chest and place them over your heart space. Take a few moments to connect with the energy of the heart. Breathe slowly and deeply from the heart space. You can keep your hands there if it is comfortable to do so, or rest them back down if not.

Step two: Now bring to mind someone in your life who you are truly grateful for. It could be a child, a friend, a family member or a partner. Just allow someone to come to mind and really feel the gratitude, love and support you feel for them. Feel it in your heart. Silently repeat in your mind 'thank you, I love you' and direct that energy towards that person.

Step three: Next, bring to mind an experience from the past you are really grateful for. Viscerally feel the love, happiness, calm or peace you felt in that moment. Where were you? Was anyone else there? Allow the feelings of gratitude from that experience to be felt fully in your heart. This might be an event from yesterday or from some time ago. Silently repeat 'thank you, I love you' and direct that energy to that past experience.

Step four: Now bring to mind an experience you are yet to experience. It might be something you have planned coming up or something you are working towards or dreaming of. Really feel what it is going to be like to experience it. Feel the gratitude, excitement and love right here in this moment. Feel a sense of gratitude for all that's yet to come. It might be the day coming up or sometime in the future. Silently repeat 'thank you, I love you' and direct that energy to that future experience.

Close: Take a deep breath into your heart and peel your hands away from the heart in a receptive motion. Smile, before you open your eyes. You might like to jot down who or what you were grateful for or perhaps a few other things that have come to mind.

Reflection

Years ago, three friends and I started a gratitude group on WhatsApp after identifying that each of us felt like we were spiralling into a rut of our own kind. We committed to messaging each other three things we were grateful for from the day before, every morning for the next month. At first, the practice felt like a huge ship leaving the dock – slow and required a lot of effort! But once we'd got going, it felt like it was in full flow and difficult to stop. A month turned into another month, then another, until we decided we'd continue for the remainder of that year. It was such a beautiful practice to share with others. Our small, trusted and intimate group gave us a sense of daily accountability and trust, but also allowed the privilege of sharing in each other's simple, magical and challenging daily events. It was so simple. Just three things, every day, that we were grateful for. But it was magic.

MINDFUL EATING MEDITATION
Feed Your Life with Love

People tend to think mindful eating is merely about being present with the food you eat as you're eating. This is one part of the practice. But the scope of the practice dives much deeper than that.

I see a mindful eating practice as a form of self-care and a way of honouring our intimate relationship with the earth. A mindful eating practice encourages us to see the bigger picture, to consider the journey the food we consume has been on, from seed to plate. Who or what was involved in the growing, shipping and selling? The practice encourages us to consider, and improve, the quality of the food we purchase and consume, and to consider if our choices are aligned with our deepest values. Mindful eating practices also help us to find the present moment and savour the absolute pleasure of food, to be present with the food you are eating, as you are eating. It can also act as a practice to understand yourself and your unconscious impulses with more clarity, through the non-judgemental observation of what emotional state you are in when you reach for certain foods, and the manner in which you eat them.

There are no rules to follow with a mindful eating practice. It's not a diet or an eating plan. It is merely about presence, awareness and consideration with an overlooked activity that most of us will do a few times a day. The opposite of mindful eating is sometimes referred to as distracted eating. You know, when you've eaten a whole bar of chocolate or a big bag of crisps without realising! Or when you eat your lunch at your desk, multitasking, not really tasting or enjoying the food you're eating at all. Pairing mindfulness with eating in this way is such a powerful combination

Benefits: *Promotes more conscious eating; improves digestion; improves sense of self-awareness; increases enjoyment of food*

Key features: *Being present with the food you eat as you're eating, and being conscious of the origin and quality of the food we choose*

Length: *Duration of each meal or snack*

Frequency: *Daily*

Tools: *None*

Best practised: *When we're too busy to or are in a rush!*

because the foundational elements of mindfulness are non-judgement, compassion and kindness. So often when it comes to food, eating habits or our view of our own bodies we are quite critical. There is no room for shame or guilt in a mindful eating practice.

Research also shows that a mindful eating practice can lead to greater psychological wellbeing, a greater sense of satisfaction and pleasure whilst eating and an improvement in body image. Mindful eating is a practice of love.

How to practise this meditation at home

Prepare: Pick one meal a day where you intend to practise mindful eating. Perhaps you tend to eat breakfast on the go or your lunch at your desk. Perhaps you tend to eat dinner in front of the TV. Pick one meal a day and set the intention to practise for at least one week.

Step one: Pause to notice your emotional state before you start eating. How are you feeling? How hungry are you? How do you feel in your body? Anchor into the present moment by engaging all your senses before you begin to eat.

Step two: Pause to engage your eyes in the eating process. Notice the colours and the textures. Spend a few moments really noticing what you are about to eat and allow yourself to reflect on the journey of the food from origin to your plate. Acknowledge the planting, growing, production and travel and all those involved in allowing this piece of food to be yours.

Step three: Notice any strong or subtle smells. Watch how your body reacts to any aromas, perhaps taste buds are activated or your tummy starts to call.

Step four: Savour the first, and every, bite. Take your time to notice the changing flavours as you chew. Chew slowly and thoroughly. Really give yourself permission to enjoy the sensual experience of eating. What a gift and a pleasure it can be.

Step five: Be present and aware of how you feel during the eating process. Avoid the urge to multi-task and just be present with the food you are eating.

Close: Stop when you're full, and give gratitude for what you have eaten.

Reflection

My second book, *Mind and Bowl* dives deep into all things mindful eating, and yet I still need to consciously practise. I took a break from writing and sat for a few moments with my face, eyes closed, in the sun, as I felt the call for a little snack. I selected plump, juicy grapes from the fridge and gave them my full attention. As I washed them, holding a full bunch on the branch, I reflected on the journey they had been on to make it into my kitchen, and all those involved in that journey. I picked one and took a few moments to notice the perfect imperfection of vibrant colour before I took a bite. I allowed the sweet juice of the tiny fruit to swill around my mouth. How decadent it felt, savouring every bite. What a shame, I thought, that I deny myself this pleasure when I eat meals and snack mindlessly. Food can give us so much pleasure, and how fortunate that we can engage with food this way and call it meditation!

ATTUNING TO CYCLES MEDITATION
Honour Change

Everything in life is in a constant state of change. Some things we want to hold on to and make them last for eternity, while for other things, change can't come quickly enough. There seems to be a certain rhythm and cycle that all things in the natural world attune to: from a fortunately long journey from birth to death, to the seasonal changes the earth moves through in one year. Menstruating women are keepers of sacred monthly cycles and all humans are subjected to the daily cycle of night and day. Other than the infinite nature of time itself, it seems for all things there is a beginning, a middle and an end. Seeking ways to make this any different is futile. The magic seems to lie in remaining present enough to savour where we are so we can make space to mark the movements in life and honour the currents of change.

Buddhists believe that so much of the suffering we experience is because we are in a state of resistance to impermanence. The practice of non-attachment, Buddhism says, is the answer. We only have to look to the natural world to witness the grace, beauty and reverence of non-attachment. Honouring and celebrating the seasons was a commonplace practice within Pagan and Celtic cultures. The turning of the seasons were marked by solstices and equinoxes. The gifts offered by change become vibrant and clear when we live our lives attuned with the seasons.

Internally we experience seasons too. We can't always be 'on'. This is why the popular notion of being in pursuit of our 'best self' can sometimes be a little damaging. By our very nature we aren't designed to always be in full bloom. We too must draw into our own winters to rest and restore, before the energy of spring surges through us once more. Any creative person will tell you that it's impossible to always be creating.

Benefits: *Creates a sense of alignment, harmony and flow in life; cultivates non-attachment*

Key features: *Creating space to mark or honour the currents of change*

Length: *Variable*

Frequency: *Daily*

Tools: *None*

Best practised: *As a year-long practice attuned to the seasons*

Allowing space for a creative winter, as I like to call it, is an essential part of living a creative life. The more you resist and try to force a creative expression, the more likely the creative spark will fizzle and burn out.

So much of our lives are impacted by changes. Our bodies, our relationships, the external space we reside in, the work we do, the company we keep and even the things we take pleasure in and enjoy. Moving with the seasons and cycles of life cultivates the ability to enjoy life – to see it as a divine gift to be savoured.

How to practise this meditation at home

External practice

The seasons themselves give us a year-long meditation practice, if we choose to attune to them. Set an intention for the year ahead, no matter which month you start in, to notice, make space, to mark and honour what is. Winter naturally invites us to draw in, become reflective and rest, whilst spring brings its own energy of fertility and renewal. We can savour the long summer nights and the gentleness of autumn, as the natural world adapts and responds.

Internal practice

Prepare: Settle into a comfortable meditation position. Steady the breath. Drop in as best you know how into your meditation.

Step one: First, bring awareness to the body. Witness the changing sensations within the body. As you move through a gentle body scan notice, witness and honour the change that takes place within the body: the rhythm of breath and heartbeat, the constant renewal and regeneration of cells, the gift of having a body that gets to age.

Step two: Next, bring your awareness to the mind. Notice the impermanence of the mind: thoughts that come and go, ideas and inspiration that arrive as if from nowhere, thoughts that sometimes lead to feelings and emotions. All impermanent. All in motion and constant change. What a rich gift it is to experience it all.

Step three: Finally, notice the impermanence of the world around you: the movement of air, the movement of people, things and life always in perpetual motion. Honour the time of day that is always giving way to the next moment. Take a moment to savour the people, and experiences you get to feel right now, feeling a sense of gratitude and appreciation for it all.

Close: When you are ready, close your meditation with a deep and nourishing breath.

Reflection

For years I resisted winter. I tried to plough on with the same energy as I was used to in summer. Resisting the darkness and fighting against the cold, I almost refused to accept that winter was happening. Until one year, inspired by a call to start living in alignment with the seasons, I let go. I forgot, for a moment, about my self-imposed belief of always having to be in control, and I let nature carry me. I allowed myself to draw in, just as the short winter nights do and enter into a season of deep rest. I gave in to cosy evenings, and said no to invitations without guilt or shame. I allowed myself to become winter, and in doing so, I fell in love with it. By the end of the winter, I do still feel myself gagging for spring. But I know that by allowing myself to fully embrace winter, I will have energy and appreciation come spring.

EYE GAZING MEDITATION
Deepen Connection

Eye gazing meditation is an interpersonal practice that has roots in ancient tantric practices. It is a practice that quite simply involves intentional and uninterrupted eye contact during a meditation practice. Simple, as this is all we have to do, but deeply challenging in regards to the discomfort this one act can create within practitioners.

It is often claimed that eyes are the windows of the soul, and this meditation practice seems to prove just that. Our eyes seem to reveal the deepest truth of what we're feeling and who we are. Through continuous eye gazing, it's possible to transcend the Self and experience a deeper understanding of unity and oneness with all things.

There is a certain level of discomfort we have to be able to sit with in order to practise this, especially with a stranger. Other than with babies, or with our lovers, we rarely look deeply into another's eyes for prolonged periods of time. Eye contact can leave some feeling embarrassed or shy, so much so they can barely look into another's eyes at all. If they do, they physically display their discomfort through blushing. What is it about eye contact that people find so uncomfortable?

Yet, isn't it interesting that it is easy to hold the gaze of a baby without the slightest inclination to look away. They are so unmasked and pure that it can feel as if you're looking into the entire universe. There is a sense of vulnerability we have to accept, and intimacy we are willing to lean into, in order to practise this meditation – you might have to put yourself out of your comfort zone. So often, discomfort, vulnerability and intimacy are activities avoided by most adults today. Research

Benefits: *Promotes a heightened state of social connection and an experience of oneness; builds empathy and compassion; builds trust, self-confidence and self-awareness*

Key features: *Uninterrupted gazing into the eyes of another*

Length: *5 minutes*

Frequency: *Infrequently*

Tools: *A willing partner, or a mirror, and a timer*

Best practised: *In a group setting*

shows the ability to sit with and transcend discomfort, alongside the cultivation of compassion, is exactly what this type of meditation can help to facilitate.[4] And eye contact of any kind releases oxytocin and dopamine, those delicious feel-good hormones.

How to practise this meditation at home

This simple meditation can be practised at home with someone you trust or in a group setting in pairs, where you can find a partner to practise with. Alternatively, you can practise by yourself by staring into your own eyes in a mirror.

Prepare: Centre yourself to begin with. Take a few breaths, feel into the sensations in the body, engage your senses and see if you can land yourself into the present moment. You might want to close your eyes and go within yourself to do this. Set a timer for five minutes (or however long you have agreed to practice with your partner).

Step one: Sit or stand facing your partner, lock eyes and hold their gaze for the duration of the meditation. Notice and allow all the emotions, sensations and fidgets you feel inclined to do, to start with. You might find you giggle and that's okay. Stay connected to your breathing and notice what is happening in your mind and body as you settle into the meditation and hold your partner's gaze. You might find you move from discomfort to a more relaxed state, as your mind moves from loudly protesting to quietly humbled. Allow any emotions to come up. Tears are quite common.

Close: When the timer sounds, you can close your eyes or lower your gaze. Take a moment to re-centre yourself. It often feels right to hug your meditation partner but that is completely up to you and what feels right and comfortable for you to do.

Reflection

Packed into a café on the Costa Rican Caribbean coast, his talk started. An American spiritual teacher who worked with Buddhist monks and huge corporate clients alike had come to town. I had no idea who he was but was told this talk wasn't to be missed. His long hair reached down his slim, tall frame almost to his waist. His well-worn T-shirt, board shorts and flip flops blended him seamlessly in with the surf town crowd gathered there to see him. He began passionately speaking of inner freedom and liberation, of freeing ourselves from the cages of the mind and falling in love with the present moment. He drew his talk to a close and instructed us to turn to the person next to us and to stare, uninterruptedly, into their eyes for five minutes. Sorry, what? I thought. The nervous looking woman next to me glanced at me with the same uncomfortable expression.

Reluctantly, we turned towards each other, uncomfortably close, and stared into each other's eyes. My ego was LOUD to begin with, full of discomfort, objection and embarrassment. As the time went on, it felt as if I was moving through layers of emotion, feeling vulnerable and exposed. Until eventually, it was as if I was seeing past 'me' and 'her' and instead witnessing the consciousness that was me and that was looking back at me. Tears streamed down both our faces. Once the five minutes passed, we were instructed to break the gaze with a hug and share a couple of minutes of reflection with each other. It turned out my partner had not left the house for weeks after struggling alone with her mental health. She nearly didn't come to the talk but said she was glad that she did. The meditation seemed to heal some part of both of us. Despite never knowing the woman's name or seeing her ever again, we shared something deep and powerful that I will always carry with me.

MORNING RITUAL MEDITATION
Anchor into Your Day

Morning routines have an ancient lineage but the popularisation of the practice has boomed since scientific research has begun to prove its benefits. From spiritual gurus to CEOs, it seems everyone is talking about a morning routine perhaps because of the links to success as well as wellbeing.

You are likely already engaging in a morning routine of some sort, probably without realising it. Perhaps the first thing you do every morning is put the kettle on to make a cup of tea. Perhaps you walk straight into the shower and begin your day that way. The difference between a routine and a ritual is that a ritual is performed consciously, with intention, presence and purpose, whereas a routine is something we can move through unknowingly on autopilot.

Starting every morning with a simple meditation ritual sets your day up with meaning, and can anchor you in any intention you wish to practise throughout the day, whether that's to embody mindfulness or practise a beginner's mind.

There are thousands of people selling their own magical morning formulas in books and on social media. Some suggest that exercising immediately is the key, others champion getting outside in direct sunlight within the first five minutes of waking. Others suggest practising yoga, journaling, an ice bath or waking at 5am. You name it, there is someone claiming that their morning ritual is *the* morning ritual that will change your life. Play with the ideas that are offered but make sure you design something that is truly right for you. You might like to ask yourself, what would feel nourishing, anchoring and feasible for you? Let your ritual be fluid too. It can change and adapt as you and your life change and adapt.

Benefits: *Setting the day up for mindfulness; increases sense of wellbeing*

Key features: *Consciously repeating a rehearsed set of actions in a deliberate and intentional way to start your day*

Length: *Any that suits you and your life*

Frequency: *Every morning*

Tools: *The tools you use will be specific to you*

Best practised: *As soon as you wake up*

How to practise this meditation at home

Decide on a practice

Perhaps for you it will be something as simple as a cup of tea outside alone first thing in the morning, to just be. Maybe it will be more detailed and formulaic, like Robin Shaman teaches in his book *The 5am Club*. He suggests waking at 5am every morning and doing 20 minutes of meditation or reflection, 20 minutes of exercise and 20 minutes of reading, studying or working with goals. Perhaps like me, your practice will be very yin in nature, slow and nurturing. Perhaps it will be very yang – straight out of bed and into an ice bath. There is no right or wrong way, only your way. Just ensure whatever it is you do choose can be performed as a meditation, through mindfulness and presence, something that can be performed consciously with intention each day. It should also feel good.

Regularity

Once you've decided on a practice, it's time to put it into practice! Set your alarm for the time you wish to or need to wake up to allow yourself enough time before your roles and responsibilities begin. All research tends to point towards the benefits of waking at the same time each day so set the intention to do just this.

Go gently

Be kind and compassionate to yourself as you begin to embed a morning ritual meditation into your life. Some people are very good at deciding to do something and then keeping it up, while others take a little longer to get into a routine. Don't let meditation be another stick to beat yourself with because some days you struggle.

Be intentional

The real challenge can sometimes come when you have managed to get yourself into some sort of rhythm, as it is easy for a conscious ritual to slip into an unconscious routine. All meditation practices, no matter what they are, are about conscious awareness, presence and alignment. A morning ritual meditation requires these three aspects for the benefits to be experienced.

Reflection

For years, my morning ritual looked the same. My alarm would sound at 5am. I would make myself a coffee, light a candle in the darkness and get back into bed. I'd pick up a pen and practice stream of consciousness journaling, whilst sipping hot coffee. I'd then move to the floor, candle still lit, cushion already laid out and I'd meditate. Then I'd try and catch the sunrise with my dog on the beach. My ritual was unhurried and untimed. It didn't feel like a tick box or like it was driven from a space of ego. It felt anchoring, nourishing and kind. But as life changed so did my morning practice. Letting it change without guilt or shame was a challenge. 'I should be', 'I should do' started echoing through my experience, berating myself for not having the time, energy or inclination to keep maintaining the same before-dawn ritual. Some days it looks more like my old 5am ritual from before. Some days, these days, my morning ritual is as simple as skin care! Taking a pause to inhale the delicious aromatherapy oils in my beautiful lotions. Eyes closed. Three centring inhales, before luxuriating in two minutes of skin care.

SURRENDER MEDITATION
Live in Trust

In many ways, all meditation practices require surrender. A yielding to and trusting in the process. It is only through surrender that we able to drop into a state of meditation. But what are we surrendering to? What is it we need to trust? The opposite of surrender is resistance, much like what is battled against in an acceptance meditation. As the saying goes, 'what we resist, persists'. In meditation, your active thinking mind that loves to be in control might resist letting go to the vast space of presence, due to a fear of the unknown or not being able to trust that space of stillness and quiet. Our nervous systems are also programmed in such a way. If your normalised operating mode is in a constant state of stress, your sympathetic nervous system (fight or flight), is always engaged and switched on. Your nervous system then can't trust that it is safe to surrender into rest and activate the parasympathetic nervous system (rest and digest). Yet it is in that state where all of the important repair work and healing takes place.

Surrender is the active turning point that leads to acceptance, healing and peace. In a lot of transpersonal approaches such as meditation, hypnosis, and even psychedelics, surrendering is the critical attribute in allowing healing to occur. Bypassing the thinking mind and allowing the body to naturally do what it knows to do. In other aspects of life, this seems to be a similar pattern too. I know a number of couples, for example, who had tried to have a baby for years, including with assisted conception treatments, only to fall pregnant once they'd given up or distracted themselves completely with something else. Surrender is a critical aspect in counselling, psychotherapy and coaching. I know from my own experience, the moment a client surrenders to the process or into our session, allowing vulnerability, not having to be in control, is the pivotal moment in our work together.

Benefits: *Cultivates a sense of trust and feeling in flow with life; improves present-moment awareness*

Key features: *Meeting your edges and soften into them*

Length: *10 minutes*

Frequency: *Daily*

Tools: *Optional – notepad and pen*

Best practised: *At times of frustration or confusion*

Surrender opens us up to receptivity. It requires a letting go of control and a letting go of the grip you might have on life being a certain way. When we want something we often grasp at it. The constant pursuit of trying is another struggle. If we give up the struggle, all that is left is what is. Surrendering to the universe allows a trust in the unfolding. Hand over the control of how something might happen and return to the present moment instead. I love the phrase 'the path to trust is trust'. Trusting in something much greater than yourself is the ultimate surrender.

How to practise this meditation at home

A surrender meditation requires you to meet your edges and to soften into them. This might be in a physical, emotional or transpersonal sense.

Prepare: Get yourself into a comfortable position lying down. Allow the body to stretch out in whatever way feels comfortable and close your eyes.

Step one: Become aware of any resistance in the body to rest. Perhaps certain muscles tense up without you noticing. Consciously soften and relax all the muscles of your body.

Step two: Become aware of any resistance in the mind to coming into stillness. See if you can sit in the seat of awareness and note what the thinking mind seeks to keep control and not let go of.

Step three: Become aware of the natural rhythm of your breathing. Witness the effortless flow of breath, something that happens all by itself without your control. Connect into the sensation of the out breath in particular and feel the energy of surrender.

Step four: If it feels comfortable to, visualise yourself in a buoyant, safe raft on a slow moving stream. Imagine yourself trying with all your might to move the raft upstream. This action represents all the ways in which you experience resistance in your life or the ways in which you're moving against the flow. Perhaps you believe you need to be up there and you work and try with all your might to get there. Meet your edge in the experience. Then imagine letting go. Giving up exhausting yourself to be in control and instead let the gentle moving stream of life carry you. Imagine lying back on the raft and being present to the changing view. Trusting that the stream will lead you to an ocean of love, peace and harmony.

Close: Carry with you that energy of relief and enjoyment found in the surrender beyond the meditation.

Reflection

Surrendering was a pivotal moment in my life changing. I was working hard, so hard. Chasing dreams, building a heart-centred business, giving a lot of time and energy to others whilst trying to make enough money to survive. Yet it started to feel like I was trying to swim upstream. I thought my goals and dreams were on the other side of effort and hard work. In my effort to control the flow, I had closed myself off to being able to receive. I was on a mission and nothing was going to stop me from getting there. This is until my body put the brakes on. A mere brush with cancerous cells was enough for me to let go of exhausting myself, to completely surrender and to take time to rest and recover. It was in that period of surrender that so many of my goals and dreams came to me, as if they were being magnetised! I realised I didn't need to work harder, make more effort or control anything at all. All that life was asking of me was to let go, surrender, to relax back into the flow of life that wanted to carry me, and enjoy the view. My goals and dreams were waiting downstream for me, after all.

CLOSING THOUGHTS

We have explored 52 practices from the deep, vast, mysterious and magical world of meditation. How did you get on? Take some time to reflect on each practice you engaged with this year. What did you learn? How did you feel? Is there a thread of intrigue tugging at you to find out more about a certain path? If you come back to this book year after year, you might find your interests, needs and preferences change. A practice you overlooked this time might well become a future favourite. Meditation is good like that, it always seems to meet you where you are.

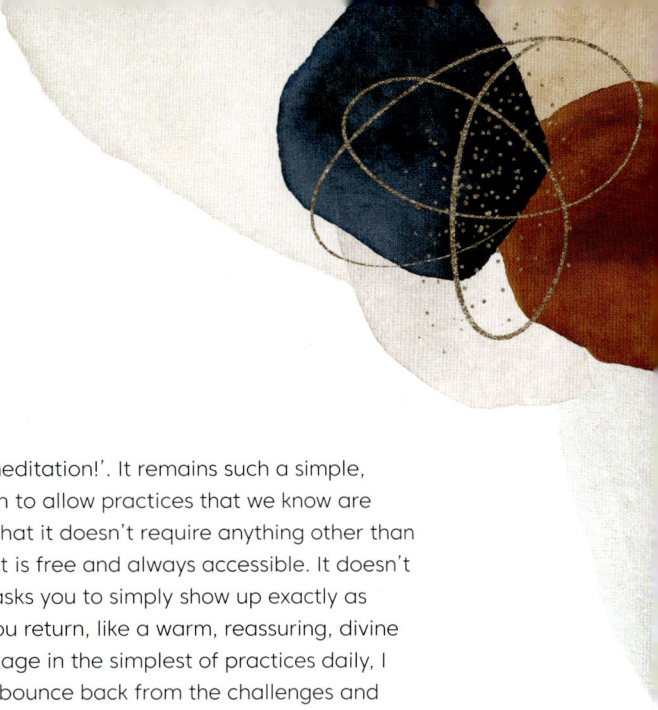

I often find myself saying 'Thank goodness for meditation!'. It remains such a simple, life-changing tool for me. Yet, it is so very human to allow practices that we know are good for us to slip. The beauty of meditation is that it doesn't require anything other than making the choice, and the time, to practice it. It is free and always accessible. It doesn't discriminate or ask you to be a certain way – it asks you to simply show up exactly as you are. Welcoming you, each and every time you return, like a warm, reassuring, divine parental embrace. When I make the time to engage in the simplest of practices daily, I know I am better able to navigate, process and bounce back from the challenges and complexities of life, and I am more likely to notice, celebrate and savour the blessings. I might not seem any different from the outside but how I experience the world, and feel on the inside, is drastically different.

Through regular practice, meditation helps us to live more fully but it's not a quick fix. It is something that, over time and continuous practice, you will start to notice a subtle, almost indescribable sensation of feeling 'different' somehow, more at peace. When people say to me they tried meditation and it 'didn't work', it makes me think of the daily practice of brushing our teeth. We don't brush our teeth once, or a few times, and expect to have clean, healthy teeth forever more. We show up every morning and night to take four minutes out of our day to tend to them. It's only over time will we notice the difference. The same can be said for meditation, yet there are so many different ways we can practise.

I hope this book has been a gentle and playful introduction to a multidimensional practice that has so much power to soothe, heal and re-energise. I hope the meditations you have engaged with have helped you to fall more in love with this wild, messy, beautiful life, and helped you to feel more whole, more you in the process. I also hope that this is just the start, or the re-start, of your relationship with meditation. There are some suggested resources on the following pages that might help you continue your journey, and I for one would love to hear how you've got on – @joeyhulin_writer.

Go gently, slow down, look up, and remember: as you are is always enough.

References

Awaken

1. C Frias, 'Shamanism & Its Basic Spiritual Function To Heal'. *Student Scholar Symposium Abstracts and Posters*, 2019: 373. https://digitalcommons.chapman.edu/cusrd_abstracts/373.

2. Sisters of Mercy, *The Breastplate of St. Patrick*, www.sistersofmercy.org/arise-celtic-saint-patrick.

3. B Rael Cahn & J Polich, 'Meditation (Vipassana) and the P3a event-related brain potential', *International Journal of Psychophysiology* 2009 72(1). doi.org/10.1016/j.ijpsycho.2008.03.013.

4. G Pagnoni, M Cekic & Y Guo, 'Thinking about Not-Thinking: Neural Correlates of Conceptual Processing during Zen Meditation'. *PLOS ONE* 2008 3(9): e3083. doi.org/10.1371/journal.pone.0003083.

5. G Perry, V Polito & W Thompson, 'Chanting Meditation Improves Mood and Social Cohesion'. Proceedings of the 14th International Conference on Music Perception and Cognition 2016.

6. J Gao, HK Leung, BWY Wu, S Skouras & H Hung Sik, 'The neurophysiological correlates of religious chanting'. *Sci Rep* 9 2019: 4262. doi.org/10.1038/s41598-019-40200-w.

7. DS Shannahoff-Khalsa, 'An introduction to Kundalini yoga meditation techniques that are specific for the treatment of psychiatric disorders'. *J Altern Complement Med.* 2004 10(1): 91-101. doi: 10.1089/ 107555304322849011.

Ground

1. ST Sinatra, DS Sinatra, SW Sinatra & G Chevalier, 'Grounding – The universal anti-inflammatory remedy.' *Biomed J.* 2023 46(1): 11-16. doi: 10.1016/j.bj.2022.12.002.

2. J Summer & Dr B Peters. 'Do Moon Phases Affect Your Sleep?', www.sleepfoundation.org/how-sleep-works/do-moon-phases-affect-sleep.

3. H Ritchie, 'Deforestation and Forest Loss', 2021, http://ourworldIndata.org.

4. A Furuyashiki, K Tabuchi, K Norikoshi, T Kobayashi & S Oriyama, 'A comparative study of the physiological and psychological effects of forest bathing (Shinrin-yoku) on working age people with and without depressive tendencies'. *Environ Health Prev Med.* 2019 24. doi: 10.1186/s12199-019-0800-1.

5. S Abookire, 'Can forest therapy enhance health and well-being?', 2020, www.health.harvard.edu/blog/can-forest-therapy-enhance-health-and-well-being-2020052919948

6. H Ling, 'Constitutional Homeopathy of the Five Elements based on Traditional Chinese Medicine.' *Acta Scientific Medical Sciences* 2020(4): 57-69. doi: 10.31080/ASMS.2020.04.0680.

7. R Zuber, W Feimer & K Fox, Schumann resonance animation, 2012, www.NASA/Goddard Space Flight Center/Conceptual Image Lab.

8. Natural History Museum, 'Nature: liberated by lockdown?', 2020, www.nhm.ac.uk/discover/nature-liberated-by-lockdown.html.

9. P Marsh, LO Diekmann, M Egerer, B Lin, A Ossola & J Kingsley, 'Where birds felt louder: The garden as a refuge during COVID-19'. *Wellbeing, Space and Society* 2021 2:100055. doi.org/10.1016/j.wss.2021.100055.

Regulate

1. Science of the Heart – Exploring the Role of the Heart in Human Performance, HeartMath Institute https://www.heartmath.org/research/.

2. A Zaccaro, A Piarulli, M Laurino, E Garbella, D Menicucci, B Neri & A Gemignani, 'How Breath-Control Can Change Your Life: A Systematic Review on Psycho-Physiological Correlates of Slow Breathing'. *Front Hum Neurosci.* 2018 7. doi: 10.3389/fnhum.2018.00353.

3. Cleveland Clinic, 2020, https://health.clevelandclinic.org/what-is-yoga-nidra.

4. TL Goldsby & ME Goldsby, 'Eastern Integrative Medicine and Ancient Sound Healing Treatments for Stress: Recent Research Advances'. *Integr Med (Encinitas).* 2020 19(6): 24-30.

5. SN Kumar, A Venu & MH Jaya, 'Effect of yoga mudras in improving the health of users: A precautionary measure practice in daily life for resisting the deadly COVID-19 disease'. *Lessons from COVID-19* 2022:41–59. doi: 10.1016/B978-0-323-99878-9.00001-7.

6. M Rangarajan & Dr. P Anandhan, 'Influence of asana pranayama with mudra on stress among hypertensive Indian paramilitary'. *International Journal of Physiology, Nutrition and Physical Education* 2018 3(2): 739-743. doi: 10.22271/journalofsport.2018.v3.i2p.2614.

7. J Nguyen & E Brymer, 'Nature-Based Guided Imagery as an Intervention for State Anxiety'. *Front Psychol.* 2018 2(9): 1858. doi: 10.3389/fpsyg.2018.01858.

8. C Aksu & D Ayar, 'The effects of visualization meditation on the depression, anxiety, stress and achievement motivation levels of nursing students'. *Nurse Education Today* 2023 120: 105618, doi.org/10.1016/j.nedt.2022.105618.

9. AD Mitchell, LE. Martin, AS Baldwin & SM Levens. 'Mindfulness-Informed Guided Imagery to Target Physical Activity: A Mixed Method Feasibility and Acceptability Pilot Study.' *Front. Psychol.* 2021 12. doi.org/10.3389/fpsyg.2021.742989.

Flow

1. Z Maurer, 'The lived experience and transformational potential of 5 Rhythms dancing meditation: An intuitive inquiry'. *Consciousness, Spirituality & Transpersonal Psychology* 2021 2: 31–46. doi.org/10.53074/cstp.2021.23.

2. J Ma, JM Williams, PG Morris & SWY Chan, 'Effectiveness of a mindful nature walking intervention on sleep quality and mood in university students during Covid-19: A randomised control study'. *Explore (NY)* 2023 19(3): 405-416. doi: 10.1016/j.explore.2022.08.004.

3. RTH Ho, JSM Chan, CW Wang, BWM Lau, KF So, LP Yuen, JST Sham & CLW Chan, 'A randomized controlled trial of qigong exercise on fatigue symptoms, functioning, and telomerase activity in persons with chronic fatigue or chronic fatigue syndrome'. *Ann Behav Med.* 2012 44(2): 160-70. doi: 10.1007/s12160-012-9381-6.

4. JM Manzaneque, FM Vera, FM Rodríguez-Peña, A Alonso & MJ Blanca 'Immunomodulatory Effects in Healthy Individuals Following a 4-Week Taoist Qigong Intervention: A Comparative Study'. *Med Sci Monit.* 2023 5;29: e940450. doi: 10.12659/MSM.940450.

5. P Huston & B McFarlane, 'Health benefits of tai chi: What is the evidence?'. *Can Fam Physician.* 2016 62(11): 881-890.

Become

1. B Shahar, O Szsepsenwol, S Zilcha-Mano, N Haim, O Zamir, S Levi-Yeshuvi & N Levit-Binnun, 'A wait-list randomized controlled trial of loving-kindness meditation programme for self-criticism'. *Clin Psychol Psychother.* 2015 22(4): 346-56. doi: 10.1002/cpp.1893.

2. CA Hutcherson, EM Seppala & JJ Gross, 'Loving-kindness meditation increases social connectedness'. *Emotion* 2018 8(5): 720–724. doi.org/10.1037/a0013237.

3. DJ Kearney, CA Malte, C McManus, ME Martinez, B Felleman & TL Simpson, 'Loving-Kindness Meditation for Posttraumatic Stress Disorder: A Pilot Study'. *Journal of Traumatic Stress* 2013 26(4): 426-434. doi.org/10.1002/jts.21832.

4. RH Morley, 'The Impact of Mindfulness Meditation and Self-Compassion on Criminal Impulsivity in a Prisoner Sample.' *J Police Crim Psych* 2018 33: 118–122. doi.org/10.1007/s11896-017-9239-8.

5. MT Bixter, SL McMichael, CJ Bunker, RM Adelman, MA Okun, KJ Grimm, O Graudejus & VSY Kwan, 'A test of a triadic conceptualization of future self-identification'. *PLOS ONE* 2020 15(11): e0242504. doi: 10.1371/journal.pone.0242504.

6. Z Dörnyei, 'Future self-guides and vision'. *The Impact of Self-Concept on Language Learning*, edited by K Csizér and M Magid (2014) doi: 10.21832/9781783092383-003.

7. D Henriksen, C Richardson & K Shack, 'Mindfulness and creativity: Implications for thinking and learning'. *Think Skills Creat.* 2020 37: 100689. doi: 10.1016/j.tsc.2020.100689.

8. S Thomaes, C Sedikides, N van den Bos, R Hutteman, & A Reijntjes, 'Happy To Be Me? Authenticity, Psychological Need Satisfaction, and Subjective Well-Being in Adolescence'. *Child Dev.* 2017 88(4): 1035–1397. doi.org/10.1111/cdev.12867.

9. O Bojuwoye, 'Integrating principles underlying ancestral spirits belief in counseling and psychotherapy'. *IFE PsychologIA: An International Journal* 2013 21(1): 74–89. hdl.handle.net/10520/EJC131392.

10. MA Cornish & NG Wade, 'A Therapeutic Model of Self-Forgiveness With Intervention Strategies for Counselors'. *Journal of Counseling & Development* 2013 93(1): 96–104. doi.org/10.1002/j.1556-6676.2015.00185.x.

Align

1. A Armstrong, 'Beginner's mind and the middle years mathematics student'. *Research in Mathematics Education* 2020 22(1): 48–66. doi.org/10.1080/14794802.2019.1647277.

2. A Chirico & A Gaggioli, 'The potential role of awe for depression: Reassembling the puzzle'. *Front. Psychol., Sec. Emotion Science* 2012 12. doi.org/10.3389/fpsyg.2021.617715.

3. S Kyeong, J Kim, DJ Kim, HE Kim & JJ Kim, 'Effects of gratitude meditation on neural network functional connectivity and brain-heart coupling'. *Sci Rep* 7. 2017: 5058. doi: 10.1038/s41598-017-05520-9.

4. VS Jordan, 'Can You See Me? Eye-Gazing: A Meditation Practice for Understanding', *Journal of Contemplative Inquiry* 2017 5(1): 7. www.digscholarship.unco.edu/joci/vol5/iss1/7.

Recommended Resources

Books

A Monk's Guide to Happiness by Geelong Thubten

A New Earth by Ekahrt Tolle

Becoming Supernatural by Dr Joe Dispenza

Blue Mind by Dr Wallace J Nichols

Breathe: The New Science of a Lost Art by James Nestors

Radical Compassion by Tara Brach

Real Happiness by Sharon Salsberg

Soul Feast by M Thompson

The Lotus and the Lily by Janet Connor

The Meditative Mind by David Goleman

The Power of Now by Eckart Tolle

The Surrender Experiment by Michael Alan Singer

The Untethered soul by Michael Alan Singer

Wherever You Go, There You Are by Jon Kabat Zin

Apps and Podcasts

Insight Timer – a free app with excellent quality meditations, courses, resources and teachers

Practice You podcast – Elena Brower

Tara Brach podcast – Tara Brach

On Being podcast – Krista Tippett

Inspire Nation podcast – Michael Sandler

Live Awake podcast – Sarah Blodin

Meditation Teachers

Ally Bogard – www.allybogard.com

Tara Brach – www.tarabrach.com

Tracee Stanley – www.traceestanley.com

Sharron Salberg – www.sharonsalzberg.com

Sarah Blondin – www.sarahblondin.com

Luke McLeod – www.lukemcleod.co

Thich Nhat Hanh – plumvillage.org/about/thich-nhat-hanh

Lynette Allen – www.awomansblessing.com

About the Author

Joey Hulin is a meditation teacher, author and poet based in Cornwall, who is making a name for herself as a thought-leader in millennial spirituality circles. She offers a down-to-earth, warm and playful approach to mindful living and spirituality. The founder of wellness company Horizon Inspired, she offers retreats, online courses, and meditations around the world, creating nourishing opportunities for people to pause and reconnect. Joey's first book *Your Spiritual Almanac* was published in September 2021 by LKP, shortly followed by *Mind & Bowl* in 2022. Her third book *Your Manifesting Year* was published by Ebury in 2023. She is an active teacher on the Insight Timer app – the world's fastest-growing meditation app with over five million users and has reached an audience of 58,000 worldwide. She is currently studying for an MA in Transpersonal Psychology.

Acknowledgements

I have said it before, and I'll say it again, I love writing books! What a joy and a pleasure the whole process is, especially when working alongside such an empowering team. A huge thank you to all at D&C, especially Lizzie, Victoria, Sam and Clare for welcoming me into the D&C family, giving me this opportunity and being brilliant to work with. Clare, especially, for working so respectfully on the edits. Thank you, as always, to my agent Jane Graham-Maw for all her guidance and support.

I have been so blessed by a range of mentors and guides, who have synchronistically crossed my path at just the right time over the years. There are too many to mention, but a special thank you to Maggie Kay for all her support early on. And my dear friends and colleagues who have walked this journey with me, especially Frida Stavenvo, Jess North, Frances Verbeek and Lisa Allen. Mel Connell, thank you for being such a supportive cheerleader over the years and for the conversation we had over dinner in The Harbour House in Flushing, which impacted the course of this book in the early days of writing it.

It has been an honour and a genuine pleasure to guide so many people through the wild and wonderful world of meditation over the last decade, through classes, courses, retreats, and now this book. During the lockdowns of 2020, I offered a free daily meditation on Instagram at 7:30am every morning. It started the week before the lockdown was announced in the UK and continued through until it was lifted. A strong community formed over those few months and I will be forever grateful to each and every one of those who attended and supported each other through such a strange and unpredictable time. From the very first series of meditation classes I ran in my living room in 2013, attended by four people, to a community of thousands who have joined me along the way – thank you. This book is for you.

Index

A DAVID AND CHARLES BOOK
© David and Charles, Ltd 2024

David and Charles is an imprint of David and Charles, Ltd,
Suite A, Tourism House, Pynes Hill, Exeter, EX2 5WS

ISBN-13: 9781446313985 paperback
ISBN-13: 9781446313992 EPUB

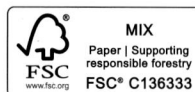

MIX
Paper | Supporting
responsible forestry
FSC® C136333

Printed in China through Asia Pacific Offset for:
David and Charles, Ltd, Suite A, Tourism House,
Pynes Hill, Exeter, EX2 5WS

10 9 8 7 6 5 4 3 2 1

Publishing Director: Ame Verso
Senior Commissioning Editor: Lizzie Kaye
Managing Publisher: Jeni Chown
Editor: Victoria Allen
Project Editor: Clare Ashton
Lead Designer: Sam Staddon
Designer: Sarah Rowntree
Pre-press Designer: Susan Reansbury
Production Manager: Beverley Richardson

David and Charles publishes high-quality books on
a wide range of subjects. For more information visit
www.davidandcharles.com.

Follow us on Instagram by searching for
@dandcbooks_wellbeing.

Layout of the digital edition of this book may vary
depending on reader hardware and display settings.